Escaping from the Prison-House of Language and
Digging for Meanings in Texts among Texts:
Metafiction and Intertextuality
in Margaret Atwood's Novels
Lady Oracle and *The Blind Assassin*

Andrea Strolz

Andrea Strolz

ESCAPING FROM THE PRISON-HOUSE OF LANGUAGE AND DIGGING FOR MEANINGS IN TEXTS AMONG TEXTS

Metafiction and Intertextuality
in Margaret Atwood's Novels *Lady Oracle*
and *The Blind Assassin*

ibidem-Verlag
Stuttgart

Bibliografische Information Der Deutschen Bibliothek

Die Deutsche Bibliothek verzeichnet diese Publikation in der Deutschen Nationalbibliografie; detaillierte bibliografische Daten sind im Internet über <http://dnb.ddb.de> abrufbar.

∞
Gedruckt auf alterungsbeständigem, säurefreien Papier
Printed on acid-free paper

ISBN-10: 3-89821-643-8
ISBN-13: 978-3-89821-643-2

© *ibidem*-Verlag
Stuttgart 2006
Alle Rechte vorbehalten

Das Werk einschließlich aller seiner Teile ist urheberrechtlich geschützt. Jede Verwertung außerhalb der engen Grenzen des Urheberrechtsgesetzes ist ohne Zustimmung des Verlages unzulässig und strafbar. Dies gilt insbesondere für Vervielfältigungen, Übersetzungen, Mikroverfilmungen und elektronische Speicherformen sowie die Einspeicherung und Verarbeitung in elektronischen Systemen.

Printed in Germany

The true story lies
among the other stories,

a mess of colours, like jumbled clothing
thrown off or away,

like hearts on marble, like syllables, like
butchers' discards.

The true story is vicious
and multiple and untrue

after all. Why do you
need it? Don't ever

ask for the true story.[1]

---

[1] Margaret Atwood, *True Stories* (New York: Simon & Schuster, 1981) 11.

TABLE OF CONTENTS

LIST OF ABBREVIATIONS 9
ACKNOWLEDGEMENTS 10
1. INTRODUCTION 12
2. THE THEORY OF METAFICTION 16
   2.1. Metafiction and/or Postmodernism 16
   2.2. The Prison-House of Language: Reality as Construct 19
   2.3. Features of Metafictional Writings 19
      2.3.1. Introductory Remarks 19
      2.3.2. The Self-Reflexive Narrator 20
      2.3.3. Implicit Features 21
         2.3.3.1. Parody 21
         2.3.3.2. The Use of Popular Literature 22
         2.3.3.3. The Use of Myths 22
         2.3.3.4. Intratextuality: Frames or Novels within Novels 23
3. THEORIES OF INTERTEXTUALITY 26
   3.1. Intertextuality and/or Postmodernism 26
   3.2. Metafiction and/or Intertextuality 26
   3.3. Preliminary Considerations and Short Historical and Theoretical Overview .. 27
   3.4. Degrees of Intertextuality 30
4. ATWOOD AND METAFICTION 34
   4.1. Entrapment in the Prison-House of Language 34
   4.2. Duplicitous Authors: Jekyll, Hyde, and "the Slippery Double" 35
   4.3. Mirror Images in Atwood's Writings 36
   4.4. The Writer as Illusionist, Artificer and Participant in Socio-Politics 39
   4.5. "The Eternal Triangle": Writer, Work, and Reader 41
5. ON THE USE OF INTERTEXTUALITY AND PREVALENT INTERTEXTS IN ATWOOD'S WORK 44
   5.1. Preliminary Considerations 44
   5.2. Mythological Woman Figures 45
      5.2.1. Introductory Remarks 45

5.2.2. The Triple Goddess 46
5.2.3. Fairy Tales and Fairy Tale Motifs 48
5.2.4. The "Rapunzel Syndrome" 49
5.3. Other Literary Inter/Texts 50
6. TEXTUAL ANALYSIS OF *LADY ORACLE* 52
6.1. Introductory Remarks on Plot and Multi-Layered Structure 52
6.1.1. Joan's Costume Gothics: Elements of Parody 55
6.1.2. Functions of Popular Romances: Escape, Compensation, or Resistance?. 59
6.1.3. Joan Foster Alias *Lady Oracle*: "Automatic Writing" and Mirror Images 64
6.1.4. The Triple Goddess 69
6.2. Reconstructing One's Past: An Overlapping of Art and Life 71
6.3. Joan Foster: "Escape Artist" 73
6.4. Intratextuality and the Merging of Fiction and Reality 75
6.5. Intertextual Relations in *Lady Oracle* 79
6.5.1. Introductory Remarks 79
6.5.2. Thomas Hardy's *Tess of the D'Urbervilles: A Pure Woman* and Double Codes of Morality 79
6.5.3. Samuel Taylor Coleridge's "The Rime of the Ancient Mariner" 80
6.5.4. Alfred Lord Tennyson's "The Lady of Shalott": Reality as Construct, Sacrificial Maidens and "The Rapunzel Syndrome" 82
6.5.5. Reel World Versus Real World: The Hollywood Film *The Red Shoes* and Andersen's *The Little Mermaid* 86
6.6. Concluding Remarks: "The Death of the Author" Joan Foster 89
7. TEXTUAL ANALYSIS OF *THE BLIND ASSASSIN* 92
7.1. Introductory Remarks on Plot and Multi-Layered Structure 92
7.1.1. Utopias, Dystopias, and Imagined Societies on the Planet Zycron 96
7.1.2. *The Blind Assassin* by Laura Chase 99
7.2. Self-Reflexive Narrators 101
7.3. Reconstructing One's Past: An Overlapping of Art and Life 104
7.4. Marys and Marthas and the Duplicity of the Author 106
7.5. Photographs: Mimetic or Distorting Mirror of Reality? 108
7.6. Foreshadowing and Epiphany 111
7.7. On the Use of Intertextuality and Intertexts 112
7.7.1. Introductory Remarks 112

    7.7.2. Washroom Graffiti 114
    7.7.3. History and/as Intertext 116
    7.7.4. Fairy Tale Motifs 118
        7.7.4.1. Sleeping Beauties in Their Rapunzel Tower 118
        7.7.4.2. The Bluebeard Theme 119
        7.7.4.3. Girls without Hands 120
    7.7.5. Samuel Taylor Coleridge's "Kubla Khan" 121
    7.7.6. Giacomo Puccini's *Turandot* 125
    7.7.7. Alfred Lord Tennyson's "Mariana in the Moated Grange" and "Break, break, break" 127
    7.7.8. Virgil's *Aeneid*: Dido's Suicide (Book IV) 130
    7.7.9. Carpet Weaving as Story Weaving: "Philomela's Artefact" 132
  7.8. Concluding Remarks 134
    7.8.1. "… only the blind are free": Freedom, Betrayal, and Guilt 134
    7.8.2. "In the beginning was the word…": Laura's "fatal, triangular bargain" . 136
8. CONCLUSION 138
9. BIBLIOGRAPHY 142
  9.1. Texts 142
    9.1.1. Texts by Margaret Atwood 142
    9.1.2. Other Texts 142
  9.2. Criticism 143
    9.2.1. Interviews with Margaret Atwood 143
    9.2.2. Criticism by Margaret Atwood 143
    9.2.3. Other Criticism 144

LIST OF ABBREVIATIONS

AG	*Alias Grace*
BA	*The Blind Assassin*
"BA"	*The Blind Assassin* by Laura Chase (embedded novel)
BH	*Bodily Harm*
CE	*Cat's Eye*
CG	*The Circle Game*
HT	*The Handmaid's Tale*
LO	*Lady Oracle*
"LO"	*Lady Oracle* by Joan Foster (embedded poems)
O&C	*Oryx and Crake*
RB	*The Robber Bride*
SW	*Second Words*

ACKNOWLEDGEMENTS

I owe many thanks to Prof. Wolfgang Zach for his continuing support. I would also like to thank Dr. Helga Ramsey-Kurz for her critical reading of the manuscript.

1. INTRODUCTION

This study analyses two novels written by Margaret Atwood, Canada's most eminent and versatile author, who is also an international celebrity and translated into more than twenty languages. As Coral Ann Howells remarks, Atwood is "the most written about Canadian writer ever", and the academic interest in her work is no longer limited to North America and Great Britain but growing in continental Europe, Australia and India (6). An expert at various genres, Atwood has written twelve novels so far: *The Edible Woman* (1969), *Surfacing* (1972), *Lady Oracle* (1976), *Life Before Man* (1979), *Bodily Harm* (1981), *The Handmaid's Tale* (1985), *Cat's Eye* (1988), *The Robber Bride* (1993), *Alias Grace* (1996), *The Blind Assassin* (2000), *Oryx and Crake* (2003), and *The Penelopiad*[2] (2005). Several of Atwood's novels were short-listed for the Booker-Prize; in 2000 *The Blind Assassin*[3] eventually won this most prestigious prize for novels in English[4]. Atwood has published numerous poetry and short story collections, including "prose poems" or "short fictions"[5], and also children's books. Among her works of non-fiction, *Survival: A Thematic Guide to Canadian Literature* (1972), which "catapulted Atwood to fame and controversy as a critic[6]" (VanSpanckeren xxi), is certainly the most famous one, and *Curious Pursuits* (2005), *Writing with Intent* (2005), and *Negotiating With the Dead* (2002), are the most recent ones. The latter extends some of her theories already postulated in 1982 in *Second Words*, a collection of some of her reviews and essays[7]. Last but not

---

[2] Atwood stated in her reading at the Goettinger Literary Festival in Germany, 22 October 2005, that she chose the title in analogy to *The Iliad*.
[3] Hereafter referred to as *BA* in the text with the appropriate page numbers.
[4] Among other prizes it also won the International Association of Crime Writers' Dashiell Hammet Award.
[5] as in *Murder in the Dark* (1983, 1984), *Good Bones* (1992), or *Good Bones and Simple Murders* (1994)
[6] In *Survival* Atwood states that the key pattern in Canadian literature is that of victimisation, which consists of four positions: denying victim status, claiming victimisation as inescapable fate, combating the victim-role, and becoming a non-victim (32-8). As she does not consider Canadian regionalism, Atwood has been accused of a "rather self-conscious single-mindedness" (Woodcock 225), and criticised for using "overtly narrow cultural definitions which represent a [...] centralist view of literature" (Hill Rigney 124).
[7] Recent editions of Atwood's reviews and essays are *Curious Pursuits* and *Writing with Intent*. Both were published in 2005.

least, Atwood is a most acclaimed visual artist[8]; she has produced a rich body of paintings and illustrated some of her own work, e.g. her poetry collection *The Journals of Susanna Moodie* (1970). Visual art is often a significant element in Atwood's fiction, to the largest extent in her novel *Cat's Eye*.

This analysis considers her Booker Prize-winning novel and one from her most creative period, the 1970s. All of Atwood's novels are – to a greater or lesser extent – concerned with the relationship between fiction and reality; they also discuss the role of art in contemporary society and the relationship between the (woman) artist and her audience. *Lady Oracle*[9] is Atwood's first novel with a strong metafictional and intertextual character, created especially by means of parodying the popular Gothic romance. *BA* can be considered a climatic achievement in regard to metafictional, structural and thematic complexity. It echoes the form of dystopian fiction already explored in *HT* and many themes the Canadian author employs in earlier novels.

At the centre of both *LO* and *BA* is a woman writer who is also the first person narrator; both artists produce different genres and describe their engagement in the writing process. The predominant subject matter in both novels is the problematic relation of art to life (or of fiction to reality). The relationship between reality and its representation is discussed explicitly, i.e. on a content level, and implicitly, i.e. on a structural level. As *BA* was published 23 years after *LO*, I will also look at differences in the author's use of metafiction and intertextuality. The framework and starting point for this analysis are recent theories of metafiction and intertextuality. I will discuss metafictional features and intertextual relations in the two novels to debate how intertextuality (incl. intratextuality) relates to metafictional issues within Atwood's work, and within *LO* and *BA* in particular. As regards the intertextual quality of *LO* and *BA*, I will concentrate on the following questions[10]: How does Atwood employ intertextual connections in the novels and how does she weave intertextual references into the novels?[11] How does Atwood facilitate the readers' recognition of the intertexts, i.e. how does she guarantee communicativity? What is

---

[8] See the studies by Sharon Rose Wilson for in-depth analyses of Atwood's visual art. Wilson stresses that Atwood's paintings introduce us to some of her prevalent intertexts and her theme of sexual politics (1996:56).
[9] Hereafter referred to as *LO* in the text with the appropriate page numbers.
[10] The terminology will be explained in chapter 3.5.
[11] I am aware that my approach to this field of research is limited, and that it is hardly possible to notice every intertextual reference in Atwood's work.

the function of intertexts and how do they relate to general metafictional issues? Do the novels also treat intertextuality as a theme, i.e. are they *meta-intertextual*?

I start with an introduction into the concepts of metafiction and intertextuality (chapters 2 and 3) before the focus shifts to metafictional features and prevalent intertexts in Atwood's work (chapters 4 and 5). The main reason for why I consider theories both of metafiction and intertextuality is that the two strands of postmodern thought are interrelated in postmodernist metafictional writings. The theoretic discussion is followed by a close analysis of the selected novels: *LO* (chapter 6) and *BA* (chapter 7). I conclude with a comparative analysis of the two writings (chapter 8).

2. THE THEORY OF METAFICTION

2.1. Metafiction and/or Postmodernism

> You can't have a thought about a stone without first seeing a stone.
> (Which leaves us in a curious position vis à vis unicorns.)[12]

Metafiction and *postmodernism/postmodernist* are notions of two literary concepts which are sometimes – and especially in regard to contemporary American fiction – used synonymously to label works of prose fiction that are self-consciously metafictional. Patricia Waugh considers metafiction a mode of writing within the broader cultural movement of postmodernism (21). However, postmodernism and metafiction can also be distinguished precisely: whereas metafiction defines a literary phenomenon which is not necessarily bound to a certain literary epoch, postmodernism roughly refers to the period after World War II[13]. Jutta Zimmermann pays attention to the fact that realistic novels, too, can exhibit metafictional features; in this case, however, their importance is only secondary (21).

The terms *postmodern* or *postmodernity* and *postmodernist* or *postmodernism* are often (conf)used interchangeably as a reference to post-war developments. Raman Selden et al. suggest employing *postmodern* or *postmodernity* for general developments within this period and reserving *postmodernist* or *postmodernism* for developments in culture and the arts, even though "this too can be made to suggest an over-simple distinction between economic and cultural realms" (201). As a relational term postmodernism[14] attacks modernism and its separation of art from life; as a revolt against the elitism of art it closes the gap between the high(brow) art of modernism and the popular art of mass culture.

The term metafiction has its origins in the American literature of last century's late 60s before it was coined in 1970 by William H. Gass in his essay "Philosophy and the Form of Fiction" (qtd. in Fogel 329; Zimmermann 3). In the widest sense, metafictional works – as the name implies – explore the theory of fiction through fiction itself to comment on their own fictional status; this can be done either

---

[12] *SW* 11
[13] Zimmermann relies on Linda Hutcheon when she says that postmodernism in Canada only starts in the 1970s (17).
[14] *Postmodernism* is dependent on a definition of *modernism*, i.e. it "denotes either a continuation of, or a radical break with, dominant features in an earlier modernism or the movements of the *avant-garde*" (Selden et al. 201).

explicitly, i.e. on a content level, or implicitly, i.e. on a structural level. A more precise definition is given by Waugh in her extensive study on the theory of metafiction:

> *Metafiction* is a term given to fictional writing which self-consciously and systematically draws attention to its status as an artefact in order to pose questions about the relationship between fiction and reality. In providing a critique of their own methods of construction, such writings not only examine the fundamental structures of narrative fiction, they also explore the possible fictionality of the world outside the literary fictional text. (2)

Currie Mark highlights the self-criticality of contemporary metafiction by defining it as "a borderline discourse, a kind of writing which places itself on the border between fiction and criticism, which takes the border as its subject" (2).

Waugh considers the growing awareness of 'meta' levels of discourse and experience in contemporary society a result of "an increased social and cultural self-consciousness" and points out that it reflects a greater awareness of "the function of language in constructing and maintaining our senses of everyday 'reality'" (3): "The simple notion that language passively reflects a coherent, meaningful, and objective world is no longer tenable. Language is an independent, self-contained system which generates its own 'meanings'" (Waugh 3). Thus, she draws attention to the strong interrelation between (post-)structuralist theories and metafiction: literary texts as pure linguistic constructs are not mimetic[15] representations of reality, for language represents and refers only to itself, i.e. to other linguistic constructs. In this sense, our knowledge of external reality is mediated through language. Metafictional writings lay bare their conventions of artifice to explore the relationship between reality and fiction.

Waugh states that "contemporary metafictional writing is both a response and a contribution to an even more thoroughgoing sense that reality or history are provisional: no longer a world of eternal verities but a series of constructions, artifices, impermanent structures" (7). This does away with the traditionally (materialist, positivist, empiricist) accepted notion of truth: "fact and fiction, story and history, truth and lie seem indistinguishable" and "constantly revise each other

---

[15] The term *mimesis* (Gr. 'imitation,' which Aristotle used in the sense of 'representation') goes back to Aristotle: "A literary work that is understood to be reproducing an external reality or any aspect of it, is described as mimetic" (Baldick 137). Mimetic criticism differentiates between truth and lie or fact and fiction.

[…]" (Schier 8), which has also led to new forms of writing, e.g. magic realism (see Waugh 9). Waugh further explains that metafiction is

> an elastic term which covers a wide range of fictions. There are those novels at one end of the spectrum which take fictionality as a theme to be explored […] whose formal self-consciousness is limited. At the centre of this spectrum are those texts that manifest the symptoms of formal and ontological insecurity but allow their deconstructions to be finally recontextualized or 'naturalized' and given a total interpretation. […] Finally, at the furthest extreme that, in rejecting realism more thoroughly, posits the world as a fabrication of competing semiotic systems which never correspond to material conditions […]. (18-9)

There are two poles of metafiction: one that accepts a substantial real world[16] and one that suggests that there can never be an escape from the 'prison-house' of language[17] and experiments at the level of the sign. In keeping with Waugh's definition, this study concerns itself with novels which can be found at the centre of this spectrum.

Baldick, too, stresses degrees of metafictionality when he says that novels discussing the writer's block are less metafictional than "works that involve a significant degree of self-consciousness about themselves as fictions, in ways that go beyond usual apologetic addresses to the reader" (133); among the latter he enumerates Laurence Sterne's *Tristram Shandy* (1760-7), John Fowles' *The French Lieutenant's Woman* (1969), and Italo Calvino's *Se una notte d'inverno un viaggatore* (1979). Important scholars who have contributed to establishing a postmodernist theory of metafiction are the discourse theoretician Michel Foucault and Jaques Derrida, the father of deconstruction. The following chapter concentrates on the medium of language in more detail.

---

[16] Waugh gives a definition of the minimum intensity of metafictionality: "The examination of fictionality, through the thematic exploration of characters 'playing roles' within fiction is the most minimal from of metafiction" (116).
[17] See chapter 2.2.

2.2. The Prison-House of Language: Reality as Construct

> What's in a name? That which we call a rose
> By any other word would smell as sweet.[18]

If unmediated experience of the external world is impossible but can only be filtered through language, novelists are imprisoned in their own medium. Fogel emphasises that "language itself is the essential property out of which the novelist makes his construct" and that metafictional writers argue against "the traditional use of prosaic language as a window onto the world" (328): "The traditional use involves the creation of characters, scenes and experiences much like the ones found in the 'real' world, which depends, in turn, on a theory of language, permitting words to act as windows" onto reality (329).

The novelist's entrapment in language is the underlying concept of all metafictional features. Metafictional writings express a mistrust of the descriptive quality of language as words cannot give a mimetic picture of reality[19]. Metafictional novelists constantly call the reader's attention to the fact that their artefacts are constructions made of words, which do not represent external reality. The focus in decoding texts must therefore shift to gaps, i.e. that which remains unsaid because it is that which language cannot represent, to a metaphoric use of language, or to certain (other) distinctive metafictional features.

2.3. Features of Metafictional Writings

2.3.1. Introductory Remarks

> The world as such cannot be 'represented'. In literary fiction it is,
> in fact, possible only to represent the discourses of that world.[20]

The novels this study analyses may be located at the centre of the spectrum of metafictionality outlined by Waugh. I will therefore only focus on metafictional features which characterise works with a 'medium intensity' of metafictionality. I will distinguish between explicit features on a content level and implicit features on a

---

[18] William Shakespeare, *Romeo and Juliet* 2.2.43-4.
[19] See chapter 3.3.
[20] Waugh 3

structural level. In summarising the respective studies by Waugh, Zimmermann, Kuester, and Fogel, one can define these features as the following:
1. Explicit Features:
    a. self-reflexive narrator
        i. dramatisation of/addresses to the reader to raise the reader's awareness of the constructed nature of the artefact[21]
        ii. discussion(s) of the writing process, the product and its reception
        iii. critical discussion(s) of the story within the story
        iv. discussion of the relationship between author, work and reader (to reflect on 'authoritative' meanings)
2. Implicit Features:
    a. rival narrators, which give different/multiple points of view
    b. the use of self-reflexive images such as mirrors or mazes
    c. intertextuality (parody and pastiche in particular)
    d. the use of myths and popular genres
    e. Chinese-box structure: the use of frames/multi-layered narratives and other intratextual features, such as the inclusion of peritextual[22] features of a text within the text, i.e. "preface", "author", "editor"

2.3.2. The Self-Reflexive Narrator

Self-reflexive narrators are an explicit feature of metafiction. Self-conscious of their role as narrators, they reflect on the writing process and argue against a mimetic representation of reality. They are aware that they are composing a work of art and discuss the problems involved in the writing process, such as word choice, plot, structure and possible endings, or reflect on the finished product, the book market, and the readership. Thus, metafictional writings may discuss not only the production of fiction, but also the product itself and its reception. Metafiction in general, and self-reflexive narrators in particular, aim at an active participation of the reader by

---

[21] versus the reader's role as 'passive consumer'
[22] The term *peritext* was coined by Gerard Genette to denote "features which literally frame a text, such as prefaces, covers, titles […]" (Allen 212).

playing with a reader's aesthetic horizon of expectations[23] and in doing so, they educate the reader. Two main theories are important in this context: reception theory and gap theory[24].

2.3.3. Implicit Features
2.3.3.1. Parody

An important metafictional feature on a textual/structural level is parody, i.e. "a mocking imitation of [...] a literary work or works" (Baldick 161). Parody is a special type of intertextual relation and thus also a metafictional tool[25]; it includes irony and exaggeration and can refer to a single text or a whole genre (as in *LO*). Parody – like intertextuality in general – implies a communicative situation between author and reader as the author assumes the reader's knowledge of certain texts and literary conventions (Zimmermann 42). Elements of parody (and irony) are an essential characteristic that define quotes as intertexts rather than sources.

In the introductory chapter to his study of *Parodic Structures in Contemporary English-Canadian Historical Novels* Martin Kuester shows that a definition of the term *parody* is dependent on the respective historical context in which it is used and he also acknowledges its relation to the concept of intertextuality. He gives an overview from Greek to Roman and from 18th-century English to contemporary theories of parody (3-23). Kuester concerns himself with "*progressive* parody", i.e. a "mechanism or modality that can be applied to any genre" and which shows "an interest in *new* modes of writing" (7, *my emphasis*). He claims that in parody "humour is a possible quality ... but not a necessary prerequisite" (3).

Linda Hutcheon states that in postmodernist parody "it is often ironic discontinuity that is revealed at the heart of continuity, difference at the heart of similarity. Parody is a perfect postmodern[ist] form, in some senses, for it

---

[23] Hans Robert Jauss, a German reception theorist, uses this term to define the criteria readers use to judge literary texts in any given period (Selden et al. 53-4).
[24] Reception theorists, such as Hans Robert Jauss and Wolfgang Iser (who differentiates between *implied reader*, who represents a function within the text, and the *actual reader*, i.e. the real person reading – or refusing to read – the text or the reading public in general), have developed models for types of readers (Selden et al. 53ff). Hutcheon favours the term *projected reader* instead of *implied reader* (see 1988:10).
[25] For a definition of parody from a strictly intertextual point of view see chapter 3.5.

paradoxically both incorporates and challenges that which it parodies" (1988:11). Kuester, who draws on Hutcheon's theory of parody, claims that "irony is, generally speaking, a structural relationship between two statements, and parody imbeds such an ironical structural relationship in an intertextual (and thus literary) context" (22). In Kuester's opinion, the intended parodic difference is especially important in the context of "the new literatures in English that have to define their own stances in opposition to a strong literary tradition stemming form the British Isles" (22). There is always an intended effect of the change or resulting difference between parodied and parodying text.

2.3.3.2. The Use of Popular Literature

Waugh considers popular literature not only "appropriate as vehicles to express the serious concerns of the present day" (86) but also stresses the advantage that a wide audience has access to and is familiar with it: "The use of popular forms in 'serious fiction' is therefore crucial for undermining narrow and rigid critical definitions of what constitutes, or is appropriately to be termed 'good literature'" (86). In this sense, postmodernist metafiction closes the gap between the high art of modernism and the popular art of mass culture.

Waugh further points out that what one age has considered trivial, another might see as "capable of expressing more profound anxieties and concerns" so that "the de-familiarization of the popular form within the new context uncovers aesthetic elements that are appropriate for expressing the serious concerns of the age" (79). Writers of metafiction may experiment with the formulaic motifs of popular literature such as those in science fiction, ghost stories, westerns, detective stories, or popular romances (Waugh 81-2). As regards Atwood's writings, intertextual references to popular art conventions parody the influence of popular literature on contemporary society, and "expectations of 'plot' in sexual relationship – a simultaneous anticipation of 'true romance' and fear of self-amputation" (Wilson 1993:xii).

2.3.3.3. The Use of Myths

Zimmermann argues that myths, an archetypal pattern of narration, can be used as metafictional tools; she states that classical myths attempt to explain certain phenomena a human being is confronted with from a naïve-logical instead of a scholarly-scientific point of view (48); therefore, the use of myths leads to a break with realistic conventions and seems adequate for metafictional purposes: *"Der Mythos bietet sich aufgrund seines archetypischen Gehalts*[26]*, d. h. der Darstellung allgemein menschlicher, universaler Konflikte in einer Welt, die von der Möglichkeit objektiver Werte und einer objektiv erfahrbaren Wirklichkeit Abstand genommen hat, als Gegenstand besonders an"* (Zimmermann 50). In her opinion, myths provide a possible imaginative framework for understanding external reality. Authors need not necessarily use myths to criticise the specific world view they express but may rather employ their structures for contemporary ideas.

However, in metafictional writings myths are often told from a new point of view[27]. They can be used to comment on contemporary society and raise awareness of structures that need to be changed. As we will see, Atwood rewrites myths about femininity from a female point of view, thereby raising awareness of patriarchal structures in society.

2.3.3.4. Intratextuality: Frames or Novels within Novels

Waugh states that contemporary fiction "foregrounds framing as a problem, examining frame procedures in the construction of the real world and of novels" to discuss what separates reality from art (28). Frames highlight "the extent to which we have become aware that neither historical experiences nor literary fiction are unmediated or unprocessed or non-linguistic" and show that there is actually no distinction between framed and unframed[28] as "content [...] will never be discovered in a 'natural' unframed state" (Waugh 30-1).

The structure of (a) novel(s) within a novel[29], which is often referred to as 'Chinese-box-structure,' can be used to explain a writer's block, aesthetic theories, or the composition of an inner novel, parts of which are often included in the outer narrative. Zimmermann points out that this technique is not restricted to literature (53-4). In the visual arts, for example, mirrors within paintings are often included to reflect the scene depicted in the painting, which stresses its artificiality. This means

---

[26] Sigmund Freud and C.G. Jung, especially, stressed the archetypal nature of myths.
[27] A very good example for this is *The Penelopiad*.
[28] Waugh states that parody and inversion function as "frame-breaks" (31).
[29] or other genres within a text

of reflection is referred to as *mise-en abyme*. Novels within novels represent a subcategory of *mise-en abyme* and create to a hierarchy in the narrative. The French writer André Gide coined the term for literary works to refer to an internal reduplication of a work or part of a work (qtd. in Baldick 138). Among the elements which can be reflected or duplicated in an embedded novel, Zimmermann enumerates story and plot, narrator and reader, and/or the style specific to a certain genre (54).

By means of their structure, multi-layered narratives stress the central conflict between fiction and reality, as an outer layer always provides the 'reality', i.e. the (realistic) framework for an embedded layer; this does not mean, however, that the narrative frame is less fictitious. The discussion of implicit metafictional features has already anticipated what needs to be explained in more detail in the following chapter.

3. THEORIES OF INTERTEXTUALITY

3.1. Intertextuality and/or Postmodernism

> As to originality, all pretensions are ludicrous, – 'there is nothing new under the sun'.[30]

Pfister states that intertextuality is "a phenomenon [...] not restricted to postmodernist writing at all" (1991:209). In fact, the term *intertextuality* is much younger than the concept it describes, according to Worton & Still, "as old as recorded human society" (2). What they mean is that any (literary) work of art is and has always been situated within a system of pre-established codes and traditions of other art forms and of culture in general; thus "the act of reading [...] plunges us into a network of textual relations" so that in order to interpret the meaning(s) of a text one must "trace those relations" (Allen 1). In this sense, meaning floats on a meta-level, in a node of *intertextual relations*.

The postmodern term *intertextuality* is sometimes used to refer to the multiplicity of references in any text and sometimes it is employed to refer to deliberate conscious references, quotations or pastiche[31]. While it is commonly agreed that intertextuality, one of the central ideas in contemporary literary theory, implies the study of textual relations (or *intertexts*) to infer meaning, there is much less agreement on how this term could provide a set of procedures for interpretation. The following chapters work out a definition applicable for the purposes of this paper by distinguishing *intertextuality* from *textuality* (as non-intertextuality).

3.2. Metafiction and/or Intertextuality

> The truth is composite, and that's a cheering thought.
> It mitigates tendencies toward autocracy.[32]

Contemporary[33] theories of metafiction and intertextuality are interconnected and overlap. I agree with Zimmermann, who argues that intertextuality can be seen as a metafictional tool (41-2). She relies on Werner Wolf's distinction between

---

[30] Lord Byron
[31] The parodic use of an author's style or of a certain type of discourse.
[32] Atwood, interview by Castro, 232
[33] With "contemporary" I mean studies which have been published in the last two decades.

Eigenmetafikation and *Fremd-* or *Allgemeinmetafikation* (qtd. in Zimmermann 40), i.e. a work of fiction self-consciously reflecting on its own fictional status versus a work of fiction reflecting on another fictional text or the relation between fiction and reality in general. The notion of intertextuality corresponds to Wolf's latter definition, i.e. fiction that self-consciously reflects on other fictional texts. It is important to note however, that intertextuality is not a feature restricted to prose fiction, but can be found in other genres – especially in postmodern drama – and that, on the other hand, not every metafictional work is also characterised by intertextuality.

Intertextuality in a narrow sense is used to describe a relation between specific literary texts and in a wider sense it relates to any type of discourse[34]. Like metafiction, postmodern theories of intertextuality have to be discussed in relation to (post)structuralism. Allen argues that "in a postmodern context intertextual codes and practices predominate because of a loss of any access to reality" (183). However, the loss of access to reality is only proposed by post-structuralists, as will be shown in the following chapter.

3.3. Preliminary Considerations and Short Historical and Theoretical Overview

Critics agree that intertextuality discusses the relationships between texts (see, for example, Pfister 1985:11). The term *intertext* is variously used for a text drawing on another text, i.e. the post-text, for a text drawn on, i.e. the pre-text, and for the resulting (intertextual) relationship between both. I suggest reserving *intertext* for the text constructed by the reader in the course of the reading process and through an analysis of the intertextual relation between pre- and post-text. An analysis of the intertextual relationship between Daniel Defoe's *Robinson Crusoe* (1719) and J. M. Coetzee's *Foe* (1986), for example, will lead to the construction of an intertext, the meaning of which depends on an intertextual relation between the two separate texts. This meaning will be different from the meanings of the respective texts considered in isolation. It is hence that the meaning we construct becomes a "foe" to the representational quality of a text.

---

[34] Baldick stresses that "the increased use of this term in modern cultural theory arises from dissatisfaction with the fixed and rather abstract term 'language' […] 'discourse' better indicates the specific contexts and relationships involved in historically produced uses of language" (59).

INTERTEXT (*RC'* ⇔ *FOE'*)
PRE-TEXT (*RC*) ⇔ POST-TEXT (*FOE*)

I am aware that this diagram is simplified because Coetzee's novel also draws on other texts – in particular on texts written by Defoe. A definition of *intertextuality* depends on a definition of *text*, a very slippery notion itself. Depending on what is regarded as text, one arrives at a wider or more restricted definition of the concept: in a wider sense, *text* can include underlying sign systems or social codes and be understood as any type of discourse or it can be restricted to "the actual wording of a written work [including audio and visual material]" (Baldick 224).

A theory of intertextuality will be more complex, the more complex the notion of *text*. On the other hand, if intertextual relationships exist between two (or more) concrete literary texts, what is the difference between intertextuality and the study of textual relationships in other literary disciplines, such as source criticism, for example? Let us investigate into the emergence of the concept at the beginning of the twentieth-century, when the linguistic turn caused a shift in paradigms, and let us consider degrees of intertextuality to answer this problem.

The notion of intertextuality has its origins in twentieth-century linguistics, particularly in the work of Ferdinand de Saussure. Saussure's studies on the arbitrary (and differential nature) of the linguistic sign resulted in a linguistic turn in the human sciences, which is one origin of the theory of intertextuality (Allen 10). It is also grounded in the literary criticism of the Russian Mikhail M. Bakhtin, who analysed literary language within its specific social contexts. Pfister argues that Bakhtin's theory is *intra*textual rather than *inter*textual for he concerns himself primarily with internal relations within a text (1985:4-5).

In 1966/7 the Bulgarian semiotician Julia Kristeva[35] attempted to combine Saussure's seminal work and Bakhtin's studies and coined the term *intertextuality* in her oft-quoted essay "*Bakhtin, le mot, le dialogue et le roman*"[36]: "Any text is constructed as a mosaic of quotations: any text is the absorption and transformation of another. The notion of intertextuality ... replaces that of intersubjectivity, and poetic language is read as the last double" (transl. by Roudiez qtd. in Müller 152).

---

[35] Kristeva discusses literature not only from a semiotic but also from a psycho-linguistic point of view.
[36] "Bakhtin, the word, the dialogue, and the novel" [my translation]

Kristeva's concept of intertextuality replaces and elaborates on Bakhtin's notion of dialogism[37]; she argues that the meaning of any literary text depends on its relation to others, as part of a genre, sign system or code. Her concept of intertextuality relates an individual work to others that have contributed to defining codes of interpretation, i.e. to the conventions that produce meaning. Her definition of intertextuality is thus indistinguishable from textuality in a wider sense: in her opinion, any text is also intertextual[38].

Kristeva is thus commonly grouped among post-structuralist critics who employ the term intertextuality to disrupt notions of stable meaning and objective interpretation. One of the leading post-structuralists is Roland Barthes, who defined any literary text as a *"chambre d'échos"* (qtd. in Müller 154), an echo-chamber or an entity which gives place to echoes of infinite pre-texts. Barthes uses a theory of intertextuality to discuss literary meaning and emphasise the role of the reader – rather than that of the god-like Author – in the production of meaning[39].

However, more appropriate for the purposes of this paper – and for the study of literature in general – are intertextual theories developed by more conventional structuralist critics, inasmuch as they argue for the possibility of decoding "definite, stable and incontrovertible" meanings in literary texts (Allen 4). Allen points out that "the different ways in which intertextuality has been used often stem from specific social and ideological agendas and perspectives" (4). Working from the margin, feminist and postcolonial critics, for example, employ intertextuality to reconsider existing power relations and notions of centre and periphery and, according to Allen, they do so "without necessarily embracing the celebration of plurality[40] and the

---

[37] Bakhtin argued that "all utterances are *dialogic*, their meaning and logic dependent upon what has previously been said and how they will be received by others" (qtd. in Allen 19). Bakhtin opposes the dialogic to the *monologic*, i.e. a fixed consensus in tradition and authoritarian societies. Like Bakhtin, Kristeva stresses that both the dialogic and the monologic poles are to be found in any text (Worton & Still 17).

[38] *"Die Entgrenzung des Textbegriffs [...] lässt das Bild eines 'Universums der Texte' entstehen, in dem die einzelnen subjektlosen Texte in einem regressum ad infinitum nur immer wieder auf andere und prinzipiell auf alle anderen verweisen, da sie ja alle nur Teil eines text général sind, der mit der Wirklichkeit und Geschichte, die immer schon 'vertextete' sind, zusammenfällt"* (Pfister 1985:9). This "the world as text"-theory corresponds to post-structuralist theories (and deconstruction in particular).

[39] In his famous essay "The Death of the Author" (1968) he claims that meaning cannot be fixed – neither by author nor reader – and that readers are liberated from the authority of the god-like Author in decoding meaning in texts, since their multi-fold interpretation of a text depends on what they have read and can therefore read into a text.

[40] By "plurality" he means plurality of the sign or *infinite semiosis*.

'death of the author'" (4). Here, Alan fails to draw a careful distinction between "author" and "Author": while it is commonly agreed that a text does not convey a theological message, a text is still a medium through which an author – a mere "scriptor," in Barthes's terminology – communicates with the reader. The God-like Author, who is "dead" according to Barthes, and who, I argue, was rather never born but a chimera fabricated by the reader, must be replaced by a scriptor-author who communicates a decoded message to a reader who has to infer meaning in (a node of intertextual relations in) a text.

To conclude, the contemporary notion of intertextuality can be divided into two positions: a wider and more radical post-structuralist position, which claims that intertextuality as a concept can be applied to all types of discourses, sign systems or codes, so that any text is part of a universal intertext, and a more restricted structuralist position, which understands intertextuality as conscious, intended, and implicitly or explicitly marked relations between two or more specific literary texts. It is the latter position which provides the underlying theoretic framework for this paper. The following chapter focuses on degrees of intertextuality and models for (inter)textual interpretation.

3.4. Degrees of Intertextuality

Various critics have tried to develop models for the interpretation of intertextual relations. The first model was developed by Gerard Genette. In *Palimpsestes: La littérature au second degré* (1982) he tried to categorise the various forms of intertextuality, distinguishing five subtypes of what he calls "transtextuality" (Müller 157ff): intertextuality, paratextuality, metatextuality, hypertextuality, and architextuality. He based his research on literature from antiquity to contemporary times, but unfortunately, with little emphasis on English literature (see Broich & Pfister xi). Müller points out that Genette is criticised for classifying his transtextual subtypes according to different criteria (159). Especially because Genette's terminology overlaps it is hardly adequate for (inter)textual interpretation[41].

---

[41] A more recent model has also been developed by Stocker (1998). As his terminology is not transparent, and especially because he does not consider the criteria of communicativity, his model shall not be discussed here.

More appropriate is a model developed by Manfred Pfister, especially because he concerns himself with intertextuality in specific literary texts. He attempted to combine the position of intertextuality in a wider sense with the more restricted one, bearing in mind that intertextuality is far from being measurable. He emphasises that his model is only a guide for differentiating intertextual relations (1985:25).

Parting from intertextuality in a wider sense, Pfister differentiates and categorises degrees of intertextuality as regards the intensity of the intertextual reference (1985:25-31). He compares this to a model of concentric circles, the centre of which is marked by the highest degree or intensity. This model makes it possible to focus on criteria which describe the intensity or degree of intertextuality by distinguishing between qualitative criteria and quantitative criteria. Pfister differentiates six qualitative categories of intertextuality: referentiality, communicativity, autoreflexivity, structurality, selectivity, and (Bakhtin's) dialogism (1985:25-30). According to Pfister a relationship between texts can be considered intertextual if it can be applied to one of the six categories.

The concept of *referentiality* helps to differentiate between intertextual relation, which are *referred to*, as opposed to influence or source, which are *mentioned*. The relationship between texts is characterised by a higher degree of intertextuality the more distinctive features of one text are incorporated in another. A quote, which is not just used, but refers to the pre-text and is distinctly signalled (or marked), so that it becomes 'meta-(pre)textual', characterises a more intense intertextual relation between pre-and post-text. According to Pfister, the post-text can interpret the pre-text both to stress its relation or distance/ difference to the pre-text[42] (1985:27).

Communicativity denotes the relationship (or dialogue) between author and reader and implies a certain degree of both the author's and the reader's awareness of the intertext, and also a degree of markedness[43] of the intertext. The highest degree of intertextuality is achieved when an author is conscious of referring to a pre-text and – by marking the intertextual reference –expects the reader to become conscious of it,

---

[42] If the post-text only stresses its relation to the pre-text, the intertextual relationship will be of a lowest intertextual intensity.
[43] An author may employ markers (or signals) of intertextuality to secure the principle of communicativity. For a detailed analysis of markedness see Helbig or Broich (31-47).

too[44]. Therefore, the reference to works of the literary (world) canon are likely to result in a higher degree of intertextuality.

Autoreflexivity is connected with the first two concepts. If an author treats intertextual references as a theme to be explored within the text, this leads to a higher degree of intertextuality, the intensity of which also depends on how explicitly (res. implicitly) the author discusses intertextuality from a meta-communicative point of view.

Structurality, refers to the syntagmatic integration of pre-texts. If a pre-text determines the structure of the post-text, this shows a maximum of intertextual intensity according to Pfister (1985:28). He gives the example of James Joyce's *Ulysses*, which is structured on Homer's *Odyssey*. The (intertextual) phenomenon of structurality is not limited to (post)modernist writings but goes back to antiquity[45].

The penultimate criterion, selectivity, defines how pointedly (an element of) the pre-text is included in the post-text. According to Pfister, a literal quotation leads to a higher degree of intertextuality than an allusion which refers to a whole pre-text or an aspect of it (1985:28). Likewise, the reference to an individual pre-text is more intertextual than the reference to conventions of a genre, motifs or myths. The more selective and pointedly the intertextual reference, the more likely this literal quotation is to take on the function of synecdoche (or *pars pro toto*).

With the sixth and last criterion Pfister leads us back to Bakhtin: *dialogism*. The stronger the semantic and ideological tension between pre-text and post-text (e.g. through irony or placing a pre-text in a different context), the higher the degree of intertextuality. On the other end of the spectrum are translations, film versions or theatre productions, which aim at an imitation of the original, and thus show a low degree of intertextuality. If all these six criteria can be applied to a text, one arrives at a text form with a maximum degree of intertextuality, i.e. parody (Pfister 1985:29).

Finally, Pfister stresses that if the focus is on individual works, authors, or literary periods, quantitative criteria have to be taken into account, too. As

---

[44] Thus, plagiarism shows a low degree of intertextuality because the author wants to conceal the source. The mere influence of other sources, of which an author might not be conscious, is of little intertextual intensity, too (Pfister 27). Let's point out that it is hard to draw the line and measure 'consciousness', though.

[45] the structural and intertextual relation between Vergil's and Homer's epics, for example (Pfister 1985:28).

quantitative criteria Pfister enumerates density and frequency of intertextual relations, and range and number of pre-texts (1985:30).

Waugh's model on degrees of metafictionality and Pfister's model on degrees of intertextuality help to draw a line between metafiction and fiction and intertextuality and textuality. They combine to form a framework for my analysis of specific features of metafiction and intertextuality in Atwood's work.

4. ATWOOD AND METAFICTION

4.1. Entrapment in the Prison-House of Language

Anyone intending to meddle with words needs blessing, ...warning.[46]

Atwood refers to the 'prison-house' of language when she says that "for any writer language is a tool, a medium, and something that limits" (interview by Castro 226). The problem any novelist has to face is the fact that "novels are ambiguous and multifaceted [...] because they attempt to grapple with what was once referred to as The Human Condition, and they do so using a medium which is notoriously slippery – namely language itself" (Atwood, "Spotty-Handed Villainesses"). Howells, too, has pointed out, that Atwood's fiction draws attention not only to the ways in which stories may be told but also to the function of language itself, i.e. "the slipperiness of words and double operation of language as symbolic representation and as an agent for changing our modes of perception" (8). She stresses that Atwood's novels are "situated at the interface between language and what we choose to call reality" and that they highlight "the artifice of representation, where the real world is transformed and reinvented within the imaginative spaces of fiction" (162). Atwood herself stresses that by studying fiction, readers "might gain more insight into how they themselves are fictionalising" and into "what is really fiction, that is, what they've made up about other people and what is really real, that is, what is really there" (interview by Metzler 149).

Atwood points out that *"how* you write about something interacts with what you are writing about and is finally inseparable from what you are saying" (qtd. in Ljungberg 12). For an analysis of her fiction it is therefore important to pay close attention to structure and narrative technique. Various critics have already noted that the designs of Atwood's narratives mirror the contents in various forms (see Ljungberg 20, for example). Ljungberg states that "the narrative tangled labyrinth" in *LO* "mirrors both the messiness of the narrator's life and the gothic maze of her own fiction" (Ljungberg 21).

Atwood's frequent use of irony in her first-person and also third-person narratives is another feature which requires close attention. Readers have to become detectives in decoding texts, and – analysing Atwood's novels – they will come to the

---

[46] *BA* 41

conclusion that truth resides in what is left out, for Atwood "never pretends that words and stories offer an unproblematic access to the real world. Instead there are always gaps to be negotiated by the characters in her novels and also by the reader" (Howells 8).

All of Atwood's novels have paid attention to the fact that truth resides in what is left out. In *BA*, for example, the self-reflexive narrator Iris remarks that language does not represent external reality when she says that "the living bird is not its labelled bones" (*BA* 395):

> I look back over what I've written and I know it's wrong, not because of what I've set down, but because of what I've omitted. What isn't there has a presence, like the absence of light. You want the truth, of course. You want me to put two and two together. But two and two doesn't necessarily get you the truth. Two and two equals a voice outside the window. Two and two equals the wind. The living bird is not its labelled bones. (*BA* 395)

The following chapter relates this problem to the notion of the author.

4.2. Duplicitous Authors: Jekyll, Hyde, and "the Slippery Double"

> Writing [...] is bringing the dead to life and giving voices to those who lack them so that they may speak for themselves. It is not "expressing yourself".[47]

In the chapter "*Duplicity*: The jekyll hand, the hyde hand, and the slippery double" within *Negotiating with the Dead* Atwood reflects on the duplicity of the author and implicitly, on the distinction between implied author[48] and real person. She emphasises that the writing self (the author) is different from the living self (the person). Atwood raises the question whether an author can be said to exist "apart from the work and the name attached to it": "The authorial part – the part that is out there in the world, the only part that may survive death – is not flesh and blood, not a real human being. And who is the writing 'I'? [...] who is in control of that hand at the moment of writing?" (*Negotiating* 45).

---

[47] *SW* 347-8
[48] A term coined by Wayne C. Booth in *The Rhetoric of Fiction* (1961). A text's "authorial voice", i.e. the real author's "official scribe or second self, whom the reader invents by deduction from the attitudes articulated in the fiction" (Selden et al. 22).

Atwood believes that "we are still living in the shadow cast by the Romantic movement, or in the fragments of that shadow" (*Negotiating* xxvi): "it was the Romantics, *par excellence*, who fixed [...] doubleness in the popular consciousness as a thing to be expected [...] above all of artists" (*Negotiating* 32). She further argues that "the mere act of writing splits the self into two" and that "all writers are double for the simple reason that you can never actually meet the author of the book you have just read" (*Negotiating* 37). Thus, "on the fate of one [half] depends the fate of the other" (*Negotiating* 38). Like Dr Jekyll and Mr Hyde[49], these double figures share their mortality, for "the double may be shadowy, but it is also indispensable" and thus "one cannot exist without the other" (*Negotiating* 37; 42). They are "two locked caskets, of which each contains the key to the other" (Isak Dinesen qtd. in *Negotiating* 54).

The women artists in the novels *LO* and *BA* are literal examples of the duplicity of the author. In *LO* the first-person narrator Joan incorporates both the 'real' person and her shadow figures: she is Joan Foster, née Delacourt (wife of Arthur Foster) versus Joan Foster as "Lady Oracle" (i.e. authoress of her book of poetry), or Joan Delacourt-Foster versus Louisa K. Delacourt (her *nome de plume*, author of Costume Gothics) versus Lady Oracle (writer of occult poetry). In *BA* the two sisters Iris and Laura symbolise the duplicity of the author. This becomes clear when the first-person narrator Iris says: "Laura was my left hand, and I was hers. We wrote the book together. It's a left-handed book. That's why one of us is always out of sight, whichever way you look at it" (*BA* 513). This leads into a discussion of the importance of perspective and mirror images in Atwood's writings.

4.3. Mirror Images in Atwood's Writings

Mirror images are prevalent in and central to an understanding of Atwood's work. Atwood frequently uses mirrors, reflections in water, photographs, and also eyes or

---

[49] Atwood points out that Robert Louis Stevenson's "*The Strange Case of Dr. Jekyll and Mr Hyde* [first published in 1886] owes something to old werewolf stories – the ordinary man who is transformed into a fanged madcap – but it also owes a great deal to old stories about the *Doppelgänger*" (*Negotiating* 39).

cameras as metaphors for duplicity and reflexivity[50] and to raise the readers' awareness of their conventional modes of perception. Ljungberg stresses that Atwood invites the reader "to challenge the confines of the mirror and to go through it [...] to discover different 'realities' behind its deceptively flat and clear surface world" (121). Atwood herself points to her symbolic use of mirrors used to discuss the boundary between reality and art, when she stresses that both the Lady of Shalott and Alice[51] are "mirror-gazers[52]": "the 'life' side is looking in, the art side is looking out" (*Negotiating* 56). She further states that "the act of writing" happens precisely at that moment "when Alice passes through the mirror: at that moment time itself stops, and also stretches out, and both writer and reader have all the time not in the world" (*Negotiating* 57).

Sherrill Grace points out that through eye[53] and mirror images Atwood explores "polarity, adversary positions, or power politics [...] to remind us of the alienating space between the perceiving eye and that object seen [...] or of the need to complement the sense of sight with 'another sense' and 'other knowledge'" (1981:59). She further states that Atwood's eye images "reinforce a basic mistrust of visual perception" for "like the 'I' of ego, the eye asserts priority of subject over object, of here as opposed to there" (Grace 1981:59). It is thus that "the implicit need for distance, for perspective, in order to accede to a more faithful representation of reality, subtends Atwood's discursive and narrative strategies" (Dvorak 445). In other words, readers have to be blind in order to see – a paradox, of course.

This is best explained through an analysis of one of Atwood's earliest and best-known poems. In "This Is A Photograph of Me" the author questions our conventional modes of perception (Grace 1980:19f; 1981:63-4):

THIS IS A PHOTOGRAPH OF ME
It was taken some time ago.
At first it seems to be
a smeared

---

[50] See Ljungberg (121ff) for an analysis of Atwood's poem "Tricks with Mirrors".
[51] the main character of Lewis Caroll's [pseudonym of Charles Lutwidge Dodgson] *Through the Looking Glass and What Alice Found There* (1871)
[52] Atwood points out that unlike the Lady of Shalott, Alice does not break the mirror and "thus discard the 'art' side for the hard and bright 'life' side, where the art side is doomed to die" (*Negotiating* 56). Her interpretation stresses that there is no dichotomy between art and reality but interrelation.
[53] eyes as images of insight and vision of the other

> print: blurred lines and grey flecks
> blended with the paper;...
>
> (The photograph was taken
> the day after I drowned.
>
> I am in the lake, in the center
> Of the picture, just under the surface ...
>
> but if you look long enough,
> eventually
> you will be able to see me.) (*CG* 11)

The first stanza seems to depict a photograph, i.e. a print of "blurred lines and grey flecks/ blended with paper". The second stanza introduces a paradox which deconstructs the mimetic representation of the first stanza when we hear that the speaker is dead. Grace summarises the central concern of this poem as such:

> Atwood invites us to look again with the assurance that eventually [we] will be able to see… "This is a photograph of me": this poem is a photograph of me, or like a photograph of me; this photograph or poem is like me. In other words "I" am double; I have my surfaces and depths and "you" will not "see me" unless you know how to look or how to read the analogy between photograph and me. (1981:64)

In this poem Atwood expresses that reality is not made up only of what one can see but that it includes the invisible, hidden, or buried under the surface. The whole truth is a combination of the visible and the invisible.

In *LO* and *BA* mirror images and photographs are major elements in narrative technique for they point to a distinction between art and reality, which blurs at the moment of 'entering' the mirror[54], and thus challenge our conventional modes of perception. They are also used to reflect on the idea of the mirror as a symbol of female narcissism. In *LO*, for example, mirrors symbolise the discrepancy between appearance (image) and reality in the sense of "the self as seen by others [i.e. the male gaze] and the self as known from within" (Bromberg 20). In *BA*, too, the first person narrator Iris reflects on the mirror as a symbol of female narcissism and more

---

[54] Joan Foster literally blurs this distinction during her experiments with "Automatic Writing".

precisely, on the discrepancy between the male gaze and a woman's subjective view of herself:

> I looked at myself in the mirror, wondering. What is it about me? What is it that is so besotting? The mirror was full-length: in it I tried to catch the back view of myself, but of course you never can. You can never see yourself the way you are to someone else – to a man looking at you, from behind, when you don't know – because in a mirror your own head is always cranked around over your shoulder. A coy, inviting pose. You can hold up another mirror to see the back view, but then what you see is what so many painters have loved to paint – Woman Looking In Mirror, said to be an allegory of vanity. Though it is unlikely to be vanity, but the reverse: a search for flaws. *What is it about me?* can so easily be construed as *What is wrong with me?* (*BA* 318)

Here, Iris discusses what John Berger has suggested in his influential study *Ways of Seeing* (1972). He argues that "women are split" for they both watch themselves and watch men watch them as objects, while experiencing themselves as female subjects (qtd. in Hutcheon 1993:155). Hutcheon suggests that when Atwood represents women's bodies as "vulnerable, diseased, injured, or as experiencing their own pleasure, she implicitly protests the male erotic gazing at their external form" (1993:154).

4.4. The Writer as Illusionist, Artificer and Participant in Socio-Politics

> If writing novels – and reading them – have any redeeming social value, it's probably that they force you to imagine what it's like to be somebody else. Which, increasingly, is something we all need to know.[55]
>
> If, as individuals, we now occupy 'roles' rather than 'selves', then the study of characters in novels may provide a useful model for understanding the construction of subjectivity in the world outside novels.[56]

All of Atwood's novels focus on contemporary social and political issues. Atwood has said in an interview: "I do see the novel as a vehicle for looking at society – an interface between language and what we choose to call reality, although even that is a very malleable substance" (qtd. in Howells 6). In *Survival*, more precisely in the

---

[55] *SW* 430
[56] Waugh 3

chapter "The Paralyzed Artist," Atwood discusses the situation of the Canadian artist from a post-colonial point of view. She sees a strong connection between the artist and society and argues that a writer without an audience and deprived of cultural tradition is "mutilated, paralyzed, and frozen" (*Survival* 184).

However, even though Atwood explores sexual politics[57] in contemporary (Canadian) society, she is certainly no advocate of any particular party line, especially because "in every case of party lines, reality is seen through a lens, and the lens distorts" (*Negotiating* 106). According to Woodcock, Atwood's view is that "politics is concerned with life as it ought to be, whereas imaginative literature is concerned with life as it is" (231). Howells calls Atwood's fiction an "ironic mixture of realism and fantasy, fictive artifice and moral engagement" (10). She notes the importance of a "fantasy dimension" in Atwood's writing:

> Alongside her realistic representation of modern Toronto life there exist other imagined worlds which belong to romance, fairy tale, or to her characters' obsessional private agendas. These may be worlds of escape, but they may be also fantasies which exist alongside everyday life and which absorb the neuroses of contemporary Western society. (2)

This underlines the statement Atwood puts forward in *Negotiating*, i.e. that the writer's roles as illusionist, artificer, or participant in social and political power cannot be separated from each other (91-122). Atwood stresses in *SW* that it is the task of the writer to describe and constantly re-evaluate the world we live in:

> What kind of world shall you describe for your readers? The one you can see around you, or the better one you can imagine? If only the latter, you'll be unrealistic; if only the former, despairing. But it is by the better world we can imagine that we judge the world we have. If we cease to judge this world, we may find ourselves, very quickly, in one which is infinitely worse. (332-3)

She further argues that "it isn't the writer who decides whether or not his work is relevant. Instead it's the reader" (*Negotiating* 122). This leads into a discussion of the relationship between writer, work, and reader.

---

[57] a term coined by Kate Millet in *Sexual Politics* (1970)

4.5. "The Eternal Triangle": Writer, Work, and Reader

> This is my letter to the World
> That never wrote to me....[58]
>
> Writer and audience are Siamese twins. Kill one and you run the risk of killing the other. Try to separate them, and you may simply have two half-dead people.[59]

The interpretation of texts has undergone a significant shift of emphasis: the focus was on the writer in the 18th-century before it moved on the text, to emphasise the importance of the reader as a re-creator of texts in postmodern and contemporary times. The question arises whether texts still have an inherent meaning and if the meaning of a text should be respected; to give an answer, one should distinguish between the *meaning* of a text and its *significance* for the reader, as did E. D. Hirsch, Jr. According to him, the meaning of a text, i.e. that which can be reconstructed from a historical point of view, must be differentiated from its significance, i.e. the actualisation through the reading process (or staging), which can be very different to individual readers[60] (Newton 51-6).

To decode meanings in texts, it is essential to disentangle author from artefact, the character(s), and especially from the narrator. Readers who do not pay attention to the narrative technique in Atwood's novels are "inclined to passively accept the discursive statements of Atwood's novels instead of questioning them" and thus become "guilty of 'naïve realism' for they fall into the trap of literalist patterns of reading" (Staels 5). Not paying attention to elements of parody or irony will thus lead to a 'naïve' misinterpretation of her novels.

Atwood's critical writings as well as her fiction and poetry are concerned with the role of the (female) artist and the tendency of the reading public to identify authors with their artefacts[61] (Woodcock 226). In a lecture on the connection between life and poetry Atwood says "it's a feature of our age that if you write a work of fiction, everyone assumes that the people and events in it are disguised biography – but if you write your biography, it's equally assumed you're lying your head off" ("Writing Philosophy"). She has repeatedly expressed her annoyance at being

---

[58] Emily Dickinson, "441 [This is my letter to the World]," *The Complete Poems of Emily Dickinson*, ed. Thomas H. Johnson (Boston: Brown, 1960) 211.
[59] *SW* 350
[60] Cf. the essay by the American critic Stanley Fish: "Is There a Text in This Class?" (1980).
[61] or the even more simplistic tendency to seek the author in her characters

confused with the characters in her novels: "You can't, obviously, be all of the narrators in all of your books, or else you'd be a very strange person indeed" (qtd. in Viner 5). Viner clarifies the most common assumptions:

> She is not a murderer (this in spite of writing as a murderer in *Alias Grace*). She was not bullied to within an inch of her existence by her childhood best friend (unlike the narrator of *Cat's Eye*). She is not a femme fatale about to steal your man (*The Robber Bride*), she does not have an eating disorder (*The Edible Woman*), and she is not a woman whose lover committed suicide (*Life Before Man*), nor a woman searching for her lost father (*Surfacing*). (1)

Even though Atwood has repeatedly made clear that she is not to be confused with the female characters of her novels, Maclean says in her analysis of *LO* that "this does not mean that the characters do not, at some level, represent some fragmented aspect of [Atwood's] own self" (195). She maintains that just as Joan's multiple identities are projections of various facets of her personality, Atwood's characters may very well be projections of her self, as if Atwood, "working through the medium of the novel itself," were "the real Lady Oracle" (196). While it is evident that authors – or rather texts themselves – take on the role of a kind of oracle, leaving a message for the reader to be interpreted, and that authors may even draw from their own experiences in their writings, this does not justify a biographical interpretation of the texts, and even less so an assumption of confessional or self-centred writing. In *SW* Atwood has equated art with "bringing the dead to life and giving voices to those who lack them so that they may speak for themselves. It is not 'expressing yourself'. It is opening yourself, discarding your *self*, so that the language and the world may be evoked through you" (347). According to Atwood

> the writer has about the same relation to the thing written, once that thing is finished, as fossilized dinosaur footprints have to the beast who made them. [...] The primary relationship is not between the thing written and the writer but between the thing written and the reader. The thing written may bear traces of the process that created it, and indeed it's fashionable these days to write in such traces; or it may not. (*SW* 344)

The writer and the reader do communicate but "only through the page" (*Negotiating* 125). Atwood also stresses that "each piece of writing changes the writer[62]", just like each reading process changes the reader (*SW* 345).

On her homepage[63] Atwood has offered suggestions on how to transfer a work from the writer to the reader and she (mockingly) defined the ideal reader as a person "who understands every word, every nuance, every hint, every melody, is elated when you want her/him to be, mystified on cue, enlightened ditto, gets all the jokes (if there are any), participates fully, thinks you are a Great Artist, and writes you touching letters of gratitude" ("The Rocky Road to Paper Heaven"). Atwood does not believe in universal literature, "partly because there are no truly universal readers" and she thinks that writing and reading are interconnected: "the process of reading is part of the process of writing, the necessary completion without which writing can hardly be said to exist" (*SW* 345). An author always writes for an intended reader and once the work is published, there is the reading public.

Atwood stresses the importance of the reader as a re-creator of texts when she says that "works of literature are recreated by each generation of readers, who make them new by finding fresh meanings in them" (*Negotiating* 50). She compares written literature to "a musical score, which is not itself music but becomes music when played by musicians": "the act of reading a text is like playing music and listening to it at the same time, and the reader becomes his own interpreter" (*Negotiating* 50).

Atwood often plays with the readers' expectations by offering a (first- or third-person) narrator who turns out not to have composed her own text. In *HT*, for example, the historical notes reveal that the handmaid's tales have been assembled and edited by historians about 150 years after the story must have taken place; in *LO*, too, Joan's memoir has been composed by a reporter who listened to her-story; in *BA* Laura Chase did not write her own novel at all.

---

[62] Salman Rushdie has said in a filmed interview that "writing, i.e. putting it down in words, makes you think in a certain way, more precisely than in conversation; it educates the author" (*Der Schriftsteller Salman Rushdie*, dir. Antoine Perset, 1994.)
[63] http://www.web.net/owtoad/toc.html

5. ON THE USE OF INTERTEXTUALITY AND PREVALENT INTERTEXTS IN ATWOOD'S WORK

5.1. Preliminary Considerations

In each of her novels Atwood has taken up traditional conventions of different genres, such as those of the Gothic romance (*LO*, *RB*, *BH*), of dystopian speculative fiction (*HT*, *BA*), of fairy tales (*RB*, *BA*), the spy thriller (*BH*), or the historical novel (*AG*) to subvert and reshape them, rather than to "abolish genres as such" (Ljungberg 27). Ljungberg argues that Atwood's novels "question the restrictive limitations of their respective genres and, by using them as strategies, transgress them and open up their creative potential" (29).

All of Atwood's novels are highly complex: they resemble a collage as several genres are identifiable in each narrative. Atwood uses intertexts and subtexts[64] both to engage in metafictional issues, to underline prevailing themes and images, and to de- and reconstruct persistent ideologies: "Disguising [her intertexts] with contemporary frames and concerns, she consistently rewrites them from a modern woman writer's point of view, parodying the so-called eternal truths to show their ideological content" (Ljungberg 15).

George Woodcock believes that the key to an understanding of Atwood's writings lies in her work itself:

> Her criticism is not separate from her fiction and her poetry; it is another facet of the same whole, and it constantly inter-reflects with them. Thus we can find clues that illuminate her critical insights in novels […] and in a great deal of her poetry, while her criticism, which rarely even mentions her own writings, gives us illuminating insights into her fiction and her poetry even when she is discussing with accurate judgement the work of other writers. (224)

Staels, too, considers Atwood's fiction "complementary in the sense that the author returns to a few essential concepts that she modulates in each novel" (15). Wilson points out that apart from Atwood's critical work her intertextual references are essential to an understanding of her writings for they "influence her themes, motifs,

---

[64] 'silent' texts which run parallel to the main story line

images, characterisation and structures" and "dramatise her character's movement from symbolic dismemberment to transformation" (Wilson 1996:56).

The titles of Atwood's writings often point to the text she draws on, as in *Double Persephone* (mythological character Persephone[65]), *Bluebeard's Egg*[66] ("Bluebeard"), *The Robber Bride* ("The Robber Bridegroom") or directly allude to the (fairy tale) intertext as in her poem "The Girl Without Hands".

Wilson lists five functions of Atwood's intertexts (1996:60):
1) to establish her characters' cultural contexts
2) to point to the characters' and readers' "entrapment in pre-existing patterns"
3) to deconstruct traditional patterns
4) to reflect on the frame narrative and other intertexts
5) to structure the characters' "magical" transformation[67] "from externally imposed patterns" to release

5.2. Mythological Woman Figures

5.2.1. Introductory Remarks

Atwood's novels feature female protagonists and her work is "a combination of engagement, analysis and critique of the changing fashions within feminism" (Howells 17). Atwood has said that "for a long time, men in literature have been seen as individuals, women merely as examples of a gender; perhaps it is time to take the capital W off Woman; I myself have never known an angel, a harpy, a witch or an earth mother. I've known a number of real women [...]" (*SW* 227-8). This statement explains her concern with a deconstruction of myths about Woman to focus on individual women. In an interview by Karla Hammond Atwood explains the notion of myth in the following way[68]:

> Myths mean stories, and traditional myths mean traditional stories that have been repeated frequently. The term doesn't pertain to Greek myths alone.

---

[65] Persephone was the daughter of Zeus and Demeter, abducted to the underworld by Hades and made his wife.
[66] Wilson considers this short story collection "a self-reflexive fairy-tale commentary" (1993:xi).
[67] Wilson stresses that the characteristic pattern in Atwood's fairy-tale intertexts is "a movement from fairy-tale dismemberment or cannibalism to metamorphosis and healing" (1993:xii).
[68] Atwood has been influenced by her teacher at college, myth-critic Northrop Frye.

> Grimm's Fairy Tales are just as much myth or story as anything else. But some get repeated so often in the society that they become definitive, i.e. myths of that society. Certainly Biblical ones have been very important in our society. We all know what the Bible's attitude towards women is[69]. [...] Women are interested in female religious figures now simply because we starved for them, but that doesn't mean that we should desacralize men and that women should be made sacred. ("Articulating the Mute" 114-6)

The following chapters discuss Atwood's subversion of Greek myths and fairy tale conventions in more detail (biblical myths will be considered in the analysis of *BA*).

5.2.2. The Triple Goddess

> Woman is not a poet: she is either a silent muse or she is nothing.[70]

As stated above, Atwood is noted for mythological themes in her writings, which connect her work to issues of feminism[71]. Marilyn Patton argues that in her writings Atwood has tried to come to terms with "myths about women and [...] gender relations which have been inscribed in literature"[72] (29). Patton stresses that "cultural myths about women are very much a form of 'power-politics'" inasmuch as they are "socially constructed myths about women to define, limit and disempower them" (29-31). In her opinion, such myths are therefore used to subordinate women and keep them imprisoned in a patriarchal tradition.

Atwood points out repeatedly that she has been influenced, or rather "terrified"[73] by Robert Graves' poetic theories and especially by his work *The White*

---

[69] Atwood in particular refers to the original sin 'caused by' Eve in the creation myth in the Book of Genesis.
[70] Robert Graves
[71] Her most recent work concerned with a re-telling of a myth is *The Penelopiad*.
[72] After completing her master's degree at Harvard in 1962, Atwood stayed another year to work on her Ph.D. thesis on "Nature and Power in the English Metaphysical Romance of the Nineteenth and Twentieth Centuries". A central idea in this yet unfinished work is that of "supernatural women and goddesses as manifestations of ideas about nature" (Patton 30).
[73] She was terrified because Graves "placed women right at the centre of his poetic theory, but they were to be inspirations rather than creators [...] incarnations of the White Goddess herself, alternatively loving and destructive, and men who got involved with them ran the risk of disembowelment or worse," so that a woman could only become "a decent poet [...] if she took on the attributes of the White Goddess and spent her time seducing men and doing them in" (Atwood, "Great Unexpectations" xv; see also *SW* 224).

Goddess, which she read at the age of nineteen: "For Graves, man does, woman simply is" (*SW* 224). Patton describes the White Goddess myth as "a multi-faceted myth which reflects socially constructed images of women's roles" (29). In her use of the Goddess myth Atwood explores constructed myths about women.

In *The White Goddess*, Graves characterises "Woman", using three mythological figures: Diana, the elusive Maiden figure; Venus, the goddess of love, sex and fertility; and Hecate (who is called "the Crone" by Graves), the goddess of the underworld, who presides over death and has oracular powers. In Graves' mythology the three identities constitute the Triple Goddess[74], "who is the Muse, the inspirer of poetry" and also "Nature, a goddess of cycles and seasons (*Survival* 199). Atwood states in *Survival* that the Hecate figure is predominant in Canadian literature, but "a Hecate with Venus and Diana trapped inside" (210). Characteristics of the Canadian Hecate figure are a fear of life, desire for self-control, self-suppression and control over others, and the Venus trapped inside stands for the buried organic vitality and creative energy (*Survival* 199-200). Atwood stresses that Hecate "is not sinister when viewed as part of a process [...] but she does become sinister when she is seen as the only alternative, as the whole of the range of possibilities for being female" (*Survival* 199). Summarising Graves' ideas Atwood formulates the following implications for a woman writer:

> Man is the poet, woman is the Muse, the White Goddess herself, inspiring but ultimately destroying. What about a woman who wants to be a poet? Well, it is possible, but the woman has to somehow *become* the White Goddess, acting as her incarnation and mouthpiece, and presumably behaving just as destructively. Instead of "create and be destroyed", Graves' pattern for the female artist was "create and destroy." (*SW* 224)

The frightening prospects for women artists formulated by Graves might have triggered off Atwood's attempts to recreate the Goddess myth. Ljungberg points out that since Atwood's first poetry collection *Double Persephone* (1961) this myth repeatedly appears in her writings (18).

Patton states that "Atwood's novels are written both in terms of and also 'against' the Triple Goddess" (31). Even if she may use the image to describe her female characters – who are often artists – the Triple Goddess myth is deconstructed

---

[74] Ljungberg points to frequent references to Trickster Gods in Atwood's writings: Mercury (Hermes), who is "credited with the invention of writing and language"; and Isis, "an avatar of the Great Goddess" (15).

and reconstructed in the end. According to Patton, in these new versions of the White Goddess

> Atwood condenses fears of being large and fat, fears of being powerful, fears of devouring or overpowering lovers and children, and the fear of being a writer. Finally, because she is the Triple Goddess, of multiple identities, she represents the difficulty of coming to a sense of one "true" single identity, the Self, a goal which Western culture has invoked as the great desideratum. (30-1)

Atwood's heroines all embark on a quest for identity and once they accept their multiple identities – and especially the negative or darker sides of their personalities – they achieve wholeness. As Staels mentions, Atwood criticises the 19th-century "liberal-humanist" idea of a single unified self, just as she deconstructs the idea of a possible search for fixed and authoritative meaning (5-6).

5.2.3. Fairy Tales and Fairy Tale Motifs

Wilson has discussed the author's intertextual use of fairy tales at great length and in detail in her study *Margaret Atwood's Fairy-Tale Sexual Politics*. She argues that "like the Bible and myth, fairy tales are among Atwood's most significant intertexts" (1993:6). Atwood's work shows a fascination with folk- and fairy tales and the author has said in an interview that the *Grimms' Fairy Tales* had been "the most influential book" she had ever read (interview by Sandler qtd. in Baer 24). She is especially attracted by the motif of transformation[75] or metamorphosis, which is prevalent in most fairy tales and religious stories, and by the positive images of women:

> The unexpurgated Grimm's Fairy Tales contain a number of fairy tales in which women [...] win by using their intelligence. Some people feel fairy tales are bad for women. This is true if the only ones they are referring to are those tarted-up French versions of "Cinderella" and "Bluebeard," in which the female protagonist gets rescued by her brother76. But in many of them women rather than men have the magic powers. (interview by Hammond 28)

---

[75] As her favourite tales about transformation Atwood mentions "The Juniper Tree" and "Fitcher's Feathered Bird" (Baer 24). These fairy tales are variants of the Bluebeard tale.
[76] She refers to Charles Perrault's tales here (and especially his "Bluebeard" tale).

Her work has also been influenced by Hans Christian Andersen's fairy tales and (Native American) folk tales. According to Wilson, Atwood's fictions and poems are "often feminist meta-fairy tales" inasmuch as the fairy tale intertexts foreground sexual and power politics in contemporary society (1996:56-61).

Atwood frequently uses the Bluebeard theme to discuss sexual-power politics and to deconstruct notions of a unified self. Grace points out that in her use of the Bluebeard theme Atwood draws upon the Grimm's Bluebeard tales[77] as much as the (similar) version in Béla Bartók's opera (1984:246). In the Grimm's versions Bluebeard[78] murders every wife to be able to marry her younger sister. He hides their dismembered bodies in a locked chamber of which only he has the key. Before he goes on a journey, he gives the key to every wife and forbids her to open the door. They disobey, however, each of them is shocked when she sees her dismembered sister and drops the key (or egg or flower) in a pool of her sister's blood. None of them manages to remove the blood stain and the proof of their curiosity. Only the curious – but also courageous – third sister is eventually able to trick Bluebeard and restore her murdered sisters back to life. Another important fairy tale Atwood uses to discuss 'amputation' or restrictions of women in a patriarchal society is the Grimm's "The Girl without Hands" (see chapter 7.7.4.3.).

5.2.4. The "Rapunzel Syndrome"

In *Survival* the analysis of the Triple Goddess in Canadian literature, where women "would rather be Dianas or Venuses but find themselves trapped against their will inside Hecates", leads Atwood into a discussion of the "Rapunzel Syndrome", a pattern for "realistic" novels about "normal women", which is not restricted to Canada (*Survival* 210). Drawing on the Grimm's fairy tale, she identifies four elements: Rapunzel (the main character), who has been imprisoned by a wicked witch (her mother, husband, father or grandfather), the tower (the attitudes of society, which imprison her), and the Rescuer (*Survival* 209-10). Unlike the handsome prince

---

[77] "The Robber Bridegroom" and "Fitcher's Feathered Bird"; see her short story collection *Bluebeard's Egg* (1983) and the novel *The Robber Bride* (1993).
[78] "Bluebeard-King" Henry VIII discarded every wife in favour of a new one, too.

in Grimm's fairy tale, the Rescuer in the "Rapunzel Syndrome" is "a fantasy-escape figure [...] of little substantiality, who provides [only] momentary escape" (*Survival* 209). Atwood concludes that "Rapunzel is in fact stuck in the tower and the best thing she can do is learn how to cope with it" (*Survival* 209). What is distinctly Canadian about the Rapunzel figures[79] is that they are unable to communicate or even acknowledge their emotions: "they have internalised the values of their own culture to such an extent that they have become their own prisons" and thus "*Rapunzel and the tower are the same*" in Canada (*Survival* 209).

According to Wilson, Atwood's texts are usually meta-narratives "of the female artist's transformation from patriarchal Medusa monster in Rapunzel's tower to woman artist courageous enough to draw on Medusa wisdom and touch" (1993:20). The "Rapunzel Syndrome" is an important issue in *LO* and *BA*; the central characters visualise their imprisonment by thinking of themselves as trapped in bodies which they do not recognise as theirs: Joan Foster's is distorted by her fat and Iris's by old age.

5.3. Other Literary Inter/Texts

At the Universities of Toronto and Harvard, Atwood specialised in the fields of Romantic and Victorian English literature[80]. Staels points out that Atwood has mentioned the nineteenth-century Gothic novel and sentimental Victorian romances as important influences on her writing (4). She further states that "Atwood's profound [but unfinished Ph.D.] study of mainly Victorian fantasy literature, its supernatural, grotesque and Gothic elements, and especially the Earth-Goddess image, left an important mark on her own fictional work" (Staels 4). Writings from the Victorian and Romantic period, together with Greek, biblical and fairy tale myths, are prevalent intertexts in Atwood's fiction.

According to Atwood-critic Kathryn VanSpanckeren, the reasons for Atwood's popularity are that "she mines popular culture but parodies it, appealing to the reader

---

[79] "If they fit any of Graves' categories, they are probably women who would rather be Dianas or Venuses but find themselves trapped against their will inside Hecates" (*Survival* 209).

[80] Victorian literature is the subject she "know[s] best" (Atwood in "Defying Distinctions", interview by Hammond 100).

who likes old-fashioned romance while entertaining the critic who spies allusions inside every character and act" (xix-xx). Atwood's novels reach an academic as well as a popular audience as she leaves it up to the reader how far one wants to penetrate into her work. She certainly has such a wide readership because her work can be read on different levels. The following (inter)textual analyses will dig under the surface level of two of her novels.

6. LADY ORACLE

6.1. Introductory Remarks on Plot and Multi-Layered Structure

> Every myth is a version of the truth.[81]

LO was first published in 1976, is Atwood's third novel and belongs to her third and "unnamed" period of writing[82], in which she had a baby, "thus becoming instantly warm and maternal and temporarily less attacked [by critics]" (*SW* 14). In 1982 Atwood defined *LO* in a lecture entitled "Imagined Realities in Contemporary Women's Writing" as "a realistic comic novel colliding with Gothic conventions[83]" (qtd. in Howells 65). Woodcock calls it a novel with "mock-Gothic motifs" (228). As a critique of the classic romance plot and "a romance about the dangers of romance" *LO* is certainly an anti-Gothic romance (Kolodny 94); however, in *LO* Atwood also uses Gothic conventions in her design of the narrative, so that the novel is "colliding with Gothic conventions".

According to Howells, a central feature of Gothic novels is fear: "fear of ghosts[84], women's fear of men, fear of the dark, fear of what is hidden but might leap out unexpectedly, fear of something floating around loose which lurks behind the everyday" (63). As further important features she enumerates enigmas, embedded stories, multiple narrators and shifting points of view, and "mixed genres, where fairy tale may blur into history or autobiography" in such a way that "the Gothic narrative suggests the co-existence of the everyday alongside a shadowy nightmarish world" (Howells 63-4). The "shadowy nightmarish world" is suggested right at the beginning when the narrator tells us: "I planned my death carefully; unlike my life, which meandered along from one thing to another, despite my feeble attempts to control it. [...] The trick was to disappear without a trace, leaving behind me the shadow of a corpse, a shadow everyone would mistake for solid reality" (*LO* 3). Officially

---

[81] *LO* 106
[82] This period also covers her growing involvement with human rights issues, which she considers inseparable from writing (see *SW* 14 and 281-2).
[83] Some of the earliest Gothic novels were written by women authors like Ann Radcliffe, Mary Shelley, and the Brontë sisters. Horace Walpole's *The Castle of Otranto* (1765) is commonly considered the first Gothic novel.
[84] Atwood places her use of ghosts in the tradition of Henry James, "in which the ghost that one sees is in fact a fragment of one's own self which has split off", which to her is "the most interesting kind" (qtd. in Howells 64).

pronounced dead after her faked drowning accident in Lake Ontario, Joan hides in a rented apartment in Italy and gives a retrospective account of her past.

LO has the form of a memoir novel (or fictional autobiography) and is told by Joan Foster, who writes "Costume Gothics"[85] under the pseudonym Louisa K. Delacourt and is the recent celebrity of a piece of occult prose poetry also entitled *Lady Oracle*[86]. Joan Foster describes her engagement in the writing of a work of 'serious' poetry and of popular Costume Gothics, in the course of which she is less able to distinguish between fiction and reality. The retrospective account of Joan Foster's life is also a parody of the Gothic romance and of those who write it.

Various critics have already noted the novel's metafictional quality: Howells considers *LO* "a story about storytelling, both the stories themselves and the writing process" (66); Lecker calls it "a meta-fictional exploration of a writer who writes about writing and a meta-theatrical story about a dramatist/actor who participates in and comments on the process of playing to an audience" (197). Grace pays attention to the novel's metafictional characteristics such as "self-reflexive satire or parody, the confusion between life and art or social realities and imaginative plots and a final sense of […] inconclusiveness" (1980:111-2).

The novel is divided into five parts and has a multi-layered structure consisting of interwoven frames: the outermost layer deals with Joan's time in Italy in the late 1960s, where she tells her story to the reporter whom she hit on the head with a Cinzano bottle in her refuge in Terremoto, taking him to be one of her Costume Gothic's murderous villains. The name of her hiding place, *Terremoto*, is Italian for "earthquake" and underlines the climatic erupting of Joan's real (or innermost) self and the merging of the various layers in the narrative; while Staels argues that the Italian setting can be seen as a metaphor for Joan's escape from the real world as "the South is the usual romantic setting in traditional Gothic fiction" (84), I think this is only partly true: as will be shown, it is only through Joan's complete identification with the fictional world that she can face reality. As revealed in the end, the whole narrative has been written down and thus mediated by the reporter to whom Joan tells her story to justify her faked drowning[87].

---

[85] The Costume Gothic was very popular throughout the 1960s and early 70s. Its precursor is the late eighteenth- and early nineteenth-century Gothic novel (Radway 1981:141).
[86] To facilitate differentiation, references to this embedded genre will be given as "LO".
[87] Thus, Joan has no authority over her own account (like Offred in *HT*).

The first embedded layer describes Joan's time in Terremoto after her faked drowning in Lake Ontario. Further embedded are chronological flashbacks: they start in Joan's traumatic childhood as a fat child psychologically tortured by her mother. Joan is raised in various Toronto suburbs as the only daughter of a war-bride mother, who has been forced to marry because pregnant and is now ambitious to move up the social ladder by conforming to societal norms. In protest against her mother and in defiance of the role model into which her mother attempts to have her turned, Joan eats until she swells to the size of a "beluga whale" and embodies her mother's "own failure and depression, a huge edgeless cloud of inchoate matter which refused to be shaped into anything for which [Joan's mother] could get a prize" (*LO* 76).

Joan is left an inheritance by Aunt Lou on the condition that she loses weight. After a final argument with her mother who attacks her daughter with a knife, Joan escapes to London, where she becomes a writer of formulaic Gothic romances (or "Costume Gothics", as she prefers to call them) and lives with a Polish emigrant. She leaves him for the more Byronic Arthur Foster, a socialist intellectual. Back in Toronto they get married, Joan secretly continues writing popular romances and has a best-selling volume of 'occult' prose poetry published, i.e. the "LO" poems, parts of which are also included in the novel. Joan becomes a public celebrity, has an affair with the Royal Porcupine, a "con-create poet[88]", and is blackmailed by Fraser Buchanan, a reporter who threatens to reveal her identity as writer of popular romances. Joan attempts to put an end to her constructed selves, fakes her accidental drowning with the help of her friends Sam and Marlene, and escapes to Italy.

Interwoven with Joan's memoir are extracts from her Costume Gothics. They have telling titles such as *Escape from Love*; *Love Defied*; *Love, My Ransom*; or *Stalked by Love*. The extracts from these romances in *LO* lay bare the conventions of this popular genre, and establish parallels to Joan's real life. According to Maclean, "society, then, is depicted as a series of conventions, indeed as a form of art" and "[t]raditional female roles, Atwood suggests, follow a Gothic pattern" (181). There are no clear boundaries between all the layers as Joan's fantasy world is determined by her 'real' world and vice versa. This stresses the interconnection of art and life or fictional present and fictional past, and it results in – at times hilarious – parody.

---

[88] He distinguishes between art and poetry as he wants to "put the creativity back in concrete" (*LO* 292).

Howells describes Joan as "a self-caricaturist as well as a parodist of Gothic romance conventions, as she switches between real life and fantasy roles in a continual process of double coding" (66). Joan offers different versions and aspects of her self, including her 'shadowy twins', which – taken together – construct her own subjective picture of her multiple identity and the roles she assumes in life: "There was always that shadowy twin, thin when I was fat, fat when I was thin, myself in silvery negative, with dark teeth and shining white pupils glowing in the black sunlight of that other world [...] I was more than double, I was triple, multiple [...]" (*LO* 298). Unfortunately, Joan cannot disentangle her romances and other 'constructed plots' from her real life, especially because she is always "hoping for magic transformations" to become someone she would rather be (*LO* 50).

6.1.1. Joan's Costume Gothics: Elements of Parody

In *LO* Atwood describes and parodies the writing of popular Gothic romances with the help of the character Joan Foster and her memoir. Joan constructs and is constructed by her narratives: she is an example of the way art shapes her life as much as she shapes that life into her romances and the prose poems "LO". Joan fails to disentangle her life from the formulaic romance plots she constructs and in the course of the novel Joan is less and less able to distinguish between reality and fiction until both layers merge in a climatic ending.

Joan's romances mirror her 'real' life and thus function as *mise-en abyme*. Both the discrepancy and the interconnection between Joan's real life and the fantasy world conjured up in her Costume Gothics result in parody. Joan's formulaic romances are a parody on her own life and her memoir can be seen as a parody on the genre and conventional plot of the popular romance. Ljungberg points out that in the narrative design of *LO* Atwood "explores all the devices available in Gothic fiction" (35): she uses mazes, mirrors, double identities, ghosts[89], and fear, both in Joan's memoir and in the Costume Gothics. These elements link the narratives to point to Joan's imaginative confusion between art and life.

---

[89] Her mother's "astral body" appears to Joan at significant moments in her life (see *LO* 209, 398-9). Joan eventually realises that her mother is a part of herself which she has repressed.

Once Joan has moved to London, she meets Paul, an emigrant who claims to be a Polish count. Her first reaction to his story is the feeling that she has met "a liar as compulsive and romantic as [her]self" (*LO* 177). When Paul's ambition to get his extensive work of 'serious' literature published failed[90], he became a writer of popular fiction. Now he writes nurse novels under the "improbable name of Mavis Quilp[91]" (*LO* 184), which triggers off Joan's writing of formulaic popular romances. Upon composing her Costume Gothics, Joan thinks that "if [she] could only get the clothes right, everything else would fall into line. And it did" (*LO* 188). When the publishers ask her to produce more "material", she mocks the formulaic quality of her writings: "Material, they called it, as if it came by the yard" (*LO* 188). She uses her aunt's name, Louisa K. Delacourt, as a pseudonym and "a kind of memorial to her" (*LO* 188), most likely because her aunt did not conform to the role of a conventional woman. Parts of three of her Costume Gothics are included in *LO*. The romance with the working title *Stalked by Love* mirrors Joan's memoir to a largest extent: both narratives are composed nearly simultaneously[92], they are intertwined from the very beginning and merge in the end[93].

Staels argues that *LO* is "a funhouse that multiplies reflections to infinity, a side show in which characters are enlarged or shrink to absurdities" (69). Joan, for example, can never get the shape of her identity right; her fears move from looking like "a beluga whale" or becoming "a huge featureless blur" to being a toad: "What was the use of being Princess-for-a-day if you still felt like a toad? Acted like one, too" (*LO* 289). She "either swells to the size of a grotesque creature or else she shrinks to the size of an absurdly small human being" (Staels 83).

In Joan's Costume Gothics, which describe a world dominated by patriarchal power structures, Joan identifies with her shadow self, i.e. the roles of the female victim characters, who get "stabbed or abandoned or betrayed" (*LO* 169). She also identifies with the images of victims ridiculed in the reel world, for example with the

---

[90] When Paul says he "wished to be like Tolstoy", Joan admits: "I didn't know who Tolstoy was" (*LO* 176). Later, she comments on the bookshelves in Paul's library, storing works by Sir Walter Scott, "quite a lot of that," and Dickens and Harrison Ainsworth and Wilkie Collins: "I remember the names because I subsequently read most of them" (*LO* 184). So, she seems to have developed a taste for 'serious' writers of historical novels.
[91] This is a reference to Daniel Quilp, a villainous dwarf-like character taken from Charles Dickens' *The Old Curiosity Shop* (1840-1).
[92] Joan had been working on it shortly before her faked drowning (see *LO* 31-3).
[93] See chapter 6.4. for a discussion of the intratextual relation between these two strands of plot.

whale in the Walt Disney film *The Whale Who Wanted to Sing at the Met*[94], and who was harpooned for his courage. Joan dreams about the Fat Lady at the Freak side show and, addressing the reader, she says: "You'd think I would have given this Fat Lady my own face, but it wasn't so simple. Instead she had the face of Theresa, my despised fellow-sufferer[95]" (*LO* 120). Mirroring her repressed emotions onto fictional "fellow-sufferers" and feeling with them helps Joan to feel her own emotions and to cope with her insecurities and fears.

Joan prefers to confront her problems in a fictional world and avoids facing them in reality. She does not tell Marlene that she recognises her as the tormentor in her childhood, who tied her to the bridge in the ravine once, letting her become "a living sacrifice" (*LO* 278). Joan knows if she told her, Marlene would only have "a smile of indulgence", whereas she herself would feel ashamed because "[Marlene's] was the freedom of the strong; [Joan's] guilt was the guilt of those who lose, those who can be exposed, those who fail" (*LO* 278). Considering herself a fated victim, she lives in constant fear: she fears the re-emergence of her repressed past and being found out, she fears the loss of Arthur's love, blackmail, and even being killed by some murderous villain.

Staels points out that "binary oppositions are the basis for character differentiation" in Gothic romances (91). Joan tries to characterise every man she deals with in real life by the opposition of 'hero' versus 'murderous villain' and she concludes that: "Every man I'd ever been involved with, I realized, had had two selves" (*LO* 357). Thinking about the "daffodil man", who untied her from the bridge in the ravine, Joan asks herself whether he was a romantic hero or a tyrannical villain: "Was the man who untied me a rescuer or a villain? Or, an even more baffling thought: was it possible for a man to be both at once?" (*LO* 72). Once she finds Paul's revolver, Joan immediately asks herself: "What was I doing with this madman […] and how could I get out?" (*LO* 190). Disappointed that the Royal Porcupine is acting like Chuck Brewer more and more, Joan says: "I didn't want him to become grey and multi-dimensional and complicated like everything else. Was every Heathcliff a Linton in disguise[96]?" (*LO* 328).

---

[94] The Metropolitan Opera in Sydney
[95] Theresa was another corpulent girl at Joan's high school.
[96] Heathcliff is the Byronic hero character in Emily Brontë's *Wuthering Heights* (1847). Edgar Linton is his aristocratic antagonist.

A striking example for such a dualistic personality is her father, whom Joan sees as both hero and murderer. He was a spy and assassin during World War II, and is now a doctor-anaesthetist who 'resurrects' people who committed suicide. Joan paints him as "a hero who has magical powers over people's life and death" (Staels 93). She says about him: "His position was the position of a man who has killed people and brought them back to life, though not the same ones and these mysteries are hard to communicate. [...] He was a man in a cage, like most men; but what made him different was his dabbling in lives and deaths" (*LO* 164).

Joan suspects that Arthur has something to hide, too: "Why should [he] be an exception?" (*LO* 357). But her husband does not fit into this image and Joan has to admit: "Arthur was someone I didn't know at all" (*LO* 357). That she has only seen Arthur and her whole life through the distorted lens of her popular romances becomes clear, when in the end Joan must wait in vain for her heroic 'rescuer-husband'; it also stresses the perils of transforming Gothic thinking onto real life.

At times Joan wilfully parodies the generic conventions of popular romances. Even though she knows that these codes do not coincide with the reality, from which readers (and writers) may seek to escape, she keeps blurring the boundaries between the formulaic life in her Costume Gothics and the events happening in her real life. Joan points out that Arthur disapproved of her fascination with clothes and would never dance with her; so, when she dresses up in her long dresses and jewellery behind closed doors, she imagines "a tall man in an evening dress, with an opera cloak and smoldering eyes" who would whisper: "Let me take you away. We will dance together, always" (*LO* 22). Joan feels that "it was a great temptation, despite the fact that he wasn't real" (*LO* 22).

Joan is afraid to admit that she writes popular romances for she suspects that as they are not considered a form of 'serious' literature, she would be judged by her profession and not be taken seriously, either. Joan's husband, Arthur, never finds out that she writes Costume Gothics: "When I first met him he talked a lot about wanting a woman whose mind he could respect, and I knew that if he found out I'd written *The Secret of Morgrave Manor*, he wouldn't respect mine" (*LO* 35). Furthermore, she complains: "Arthur's friends and the books he read, which always had footnotes, and the causes he took up made me feel deficient and somehow absurd, a sort of intellectual village idiot, and revealing my profession would certainly have made it worse" (*LO* 36). Just as Paul says: "I never read those trashy books by Mavis Quilp

[…] I write them" (*LO* 184f), Joan does not consider her profession to be respectable and remarks: "Usually I wrote my Costume Gothics on the typewriter, with my eyes closed. It was somehow inhibiting to have to see what I'd put on the page […]" (*LO* 156).

These statements reveal that Joan knows about the formulaic and stereotypical conventions of popular romances. Feeling the need to escape from harsh reality, she tries to transform these conventions onto her real life and assigns stereotypical character roles to the people who surround her. Her dilemma consists in failing to disentangle reality from fiction, and her own self from a vision of herself which she sees reflected in the (male) gaze of the other.

6.1.2. Functions of Popular Romances: Escape, Compensation, or Resistance?

Atwood, who is an expert in 19th-century English literature, has always been fascinated by popular (Gothic) fiction. In an interview by Hammond she raises the question why readers are fascinated by books that essentially say, "Your husband is trying to kill you" and states: "People aren't interested in pop culture books out of pure random selection. They connect with something real in people's lives" ("Defying Distinctions" 107). To sustain her argument I will look at a well-known ethnographic study on popular romances.

In *Reading the Romance: Women, Patriarchy and Popular Literature*, Janice Radway analyses popular romances and their fascination to female readers[97]. Radway considers the function of escape, compensation, and – to some extent also – resistance for the female readership. Regarding the narrative structure, Radway distinguishes between successful and failed romances. She claims that successful romances show the same underlying structure: a) the beginning situation which sets up a tension, b) an intermediate intervention, which causes and eventually explains the final transformation, and c) a final situation which brings about a transformation of the initial situation and resolves the tension.

Mick Underwood aptly summarises the formulaic plot structure of such romances:

---

[97] Her study centres on the female readership in Smithton, a Midwestern town in the USA.

Typically, the heroine is removed from her familiar surroundings, usually associated with a fairly comfortable background in childhood or family. She meets an aristocratic man whose advances she initially rejects because she believes he has only a sexual interest in her. Thus she is typically antagonistic towards him. Then the intermediate intervention occurs. Typically, heroine and hero become separated in some way. This makes possible an eventual reversal of the initial rejection and antagonism. The hero typically displays an act of tenderness which is not fully explained at this juncture, but provides the opportunity for a gradual re-interpretation of the hero's initial behaviour. Eventually, the hero declares his love for the heroine and they are happily reconciled. (see also Radway 1997:119-56)

An analysis of the plot of *LO* shows how Atwood plays with the formulaic plot line of popular romances. Joan Foster *is* removed from her familiar surroundings, but of her own account and to escape from her mother and the traumatic childhood experiences. Leaving her mother is "the formal beginning of [her] second self" (*LO* 163). Then she meets the 'aristocratic' Paul, who claims to be a Polish count and who 'rescues' her when she falls off a bus in London; Joan, however, is far from rejecting his advances and Paul feels guilty when he finds out that theirs was her first sexual encounter. Joan leaves Paul for another 'romantic Byronic hero', Arthur, whom she marries for financial reasons. When The Royal Porcupine, the next romantic hero crosses Joan's way, she starts having an affair with him,[98] which is something not granted in popular romances. Once she realises that none of her Byronic heroes is very Byronic, she states: "I never really loved anyone, not Paul, not Chuck The Royal Porcupine, not even Arthur. I'd polished them with my love and expected them to shine, brightly enough to return my own reflection, enhanced and sparkling" (*LO* 345). Joan hopes for a more comfortable reflection of herself when she looks at (a constructed love-relationship with) some romantic hero.

Radway's study shows that the female readers consider the act of reading "combative" and "compensatory":

> It is combative in the sense that it enables them to refuse the other-directed social role prescribed for them by their position within the institution of

---

[98] While Joan can 'realise' her fantasies with The Royal Porcupine, who had "opened a space-time door to the fifth dimension" (*LO* 298), she feels no need to escape into the fantasy world of her Costume Gothics: "I'd completely lost interest in the Costume Gothics. What did I need them for now?" (*LO* 302).

marriage. In picking up a book [...] they refuse temporarily their family's otherwise constant demand that they attend to the wants of others even as they act deliberately to do something for their own private pleasure. Their activity is compensatory [...] in that it permits them to focus on themselves and to carve out a solitary space within an arena where their self-interest is usually identified with the interests of others and where they are defined as a public resource to be mined at will by the family. (Radway 1997:211)

Radway argues that romances function as tranquillisers; their "short-lived therapeutical value [...] is finally the cause of its repetitive consumption" (170). Joan starts reading popular fiction to escape her unhappy war-bride-mother's ideal of her – and she finds that ideal in the romances she reads. As a child, she lives of books and food, and as an adult she lives of writing Costume Gothics – they sustain her financially and emotionally. Joan experiences escape and transformation through reading and later also writing popular fiction.

While the romance is certainly patriarchal from an ideological point of view and may even be interpreted as a recommendation of patriarchy, Radway claims that women readers –who generally know the happy endings to be illusory – might also resist such an ideology:

When the act of romance reading is viewed as it is by the readers themselves, from within a belief system that accepts as given the institutions of heterosexuality and monogamous marriage, it can be seen as an activity of mild protest and longing for reform necessitated by those institutions' failure to satisfy the emotional needs of women. (Radway 1997:213)

In *LO*, Paul, the Polish count, explains the function of "escape literature" as "an escape for the writer as well as the reader" (*LO* 186): "Nurses do not read the nurse novels. They are read by women who wish mistakenly to be a nurse. [...] If the nurses wish to avoid the problems of their lives, they must write spy stories" (*LO* 186-7). Joan not only decides to write Gothic romances to solve her financial problems, but also to escape into a world less harmful:

I was two people at once, with two sets of identification papers, two bank accounts, two different groups of people who believed I existed. I was Joan Foster [...]. But I was also Louisa K. Delacourt. As long as I could spend a certain amount of time each week as Louisa, I was all right, I was patient and forbearing, warm, a sympathetic listener. But if I was cut off, if I couldn't work at my current Gothic, I would become mean and irritable, drink too much and start to cry. (LO 257)

She needs the regular escape into a world, "where happiness [is] possible and wounds [are] only ritual ones", to assume the role that she thinks is required of her in real life (*LO* 346). However, Joan has to admit: "It was true I had two lives, but on off days I felt that neither of them was completely real" (*LO* 262). When she is alone and no longer has to live up to the ideal of womanhood prescribed by society, she realises her inner emptiness.

At high school Joan "played kindly aunt and wise-woman" to her classmates, in her opinion the only role possible for a fat girl (*LO* 108). Her 'friends' entrusted their innermost secrets to her, while she herself never showed her "hatred and jealousy" towards them, even though she was tempted to reveal herself as "the duplicitous monster" she knew herself to be (*LO* 110). Looking back on her childhood, Joan remarks: "About the only advantage of this life strain was that I gained a thorough knowledge of a portion of my future audience: those who got married too young, who had babies too early, who wanted princes and castles and ended up with cramped apartments and grudging husbands" (*LO* 110).

As Joan knows about the urge to escape from real life, she facilitates her readers' identification with the heroines: "The heroines of my books were mere stand-ins: their features were never clearly defined, their faces were putty which each reader could reshape into her own, adding a little beauty [...]. I had the power to turn [the readers] from pumpkins to pure gold" (*LO* 37). Joan's romances provide escape from her readers' brutal reality. Most importantly, however, Joan fashions her own identification with the heroines in such a way that they become her own double figures and thus an adequate means of escape for herself. Howells stresses that Joan's heroines "are all partial figurings of her fantasies of desirable femininity, while their persecutions are displacements of her own sense of inadequacy and dread" (72).

Staels argues that "in writing the commercial tales, [Joan] participates in the reproduction and maintenance of the power politics that underlies these romances" (85). Joan knows about the power politics inherent to the romances, but she is even more threatened by 'real' society's sexual-power politics; therefore, she becomes an "escape artist" (*LO* 405). She needs the escape into the world of fantasy the writing act gives her:

> These books, with their covers featuring gloomy, foreboding castles and apprehensive maidens in modified night-gowns, hair streaming in the wind, eyes bulging like those of a loiter victim, toes poised for flight, would be considered trash of the lowest order. Worse that trash, for didn't they exploit the masses, corrupt by distracting, and perpetuate degrading stereotypes of women as helpless and persecuted? They did, and I knew it, but I couldn't stop. (*LO* 36)

Joan knows about the importance of escape for her female readers but she suspects that Arthur "wouldn't have been able to understand in the least the desire, the pure quintessential need of [her] readers for escape, a thing [she herself] understood only too well" (LO 36). Furthermore, "war, politics and explorations up the Amazon, those other great escapes, were by and large denied them [...] so why refuse them their castles, their persecutors and their princes?" (*LO* 37). Joan mockingly argues that if patriarchy refuses women all "other great escapes", they should at least be allowed the only escape open to them. Joan stresses: "I dealt in hope, I offered a vision of a better world, however preposterous [...]. I couldn't see that it was much different from the visions Arthur and his friends offered, and it was just as realistic" (*LO* 38). Joan is also aware that in order to change society one has to reach society:

> So you're interested in the people, the workers, I would say to [Arthur] during my solitary midnight justifications. Well, that's what the people and the workers read, the female ones anyway, when they have time to read at all and they can't face the social realism of True Confessions. They read my books. (*LO* 38)

Joan's reflections on popular literature serve the purpose of discussing the complex interrelation between popular art and society. *LO* not only lays bare and parodies the conventions of popular romances, it also attempts to analyse the appeal of such literature for female readers. Howells notes that "we are also forced to acknowledge the limits of such conventions when borders blur between fiction and real life" (10): Atwood's women artists "are forced to confront the gap between traditional narratives of female helplessness and a far more complex reality which forces women to revise their life stories" (Howells 10). One such first attempt to revise her-story, is Joan's experiment with Automatic Writing.

6.1.3. Joan Foster Alias *Lady Oracle*: "Automatic Writing" and Mirror Images

Through "Automatic Writing" séances[99], recommended to her by Leda Sprott[100], Joan produces some mythic prose poems with "this little adventure into the extra-natural" (*LO* 271). The book's immediate success turns her into a celebrity. After the publication of her work of 'serious' literature Joan also starts to reflect on her public image, and feels more and more uncomfortable by the public's interest in her personality, because it might lead to a revelation of her past. She keeps newspaper clippings about her poems stored in her scrap-book; they focus on her appearance and describe her as looking *"like a lush Rossetti portrait"* or *"impressively Junoesque in her flowing red hair and green robe"* (*LO* 11). Joan learns that "hair in the female was regarded as more important than either talent or the lack of it" (*LO* 11), and she is faced with the discrepancy between her public image and her own view of herself:

> I felt very visible. But it was as if someone with my name were out there in the real world, impersonating me, saying things I'd never said but which appeared in the newspapers, doing things for which I had to take the consequences: my dark twin, my funhouse-mirror reflection. She was taller than I was, more beautiful, more threatening. She wanted to kill me and take my place, and by the time she did this no one would notice the difference because the media were in on the plot, they were helping her. (*LO* 304)

She has to face the fact that the reading public – with the help of the media – constructs their own image of her personality. As she is unable to draw a boundary between reality and fantasy, she even lets this other imagined persona, the dead author of "LO", materialise and feels frightened by her. Even worse, she takes the criticism on her work to be an evaluation of herself. After reading the newspaper article: *Lady Oracle*: Hoax or Delusion? (*LO* 303), she claims: "I was inept, I was slovenly and hollow, a hoax, a delusion" (*LO* 305).

Shortly after the publication of *LO* Atwood admitted in an interview by Beverly Slopen that she found her public image "quite freakish": "People project on

---

[99] Sitting in front of a triple mirror, Joan puts a lighted candle and a piece of paper in front of her, takes a pen and closes her eyes. After descending a dark corridor in a trance-like state, she has subconsciously written some words in front of her (*LO* 265ff). She compiles these words into a book of poetry and has it published after three months.

[100] Like most characters in *LO*, she has a double identity, too, and reappears as Reverend Eunece P. Revele to carry out the wedding ceremony (see *LO* 243).

me their image of what a poet should be. It bothers them that I'm not eccentric and they think up descriptions of me that make me quite poetical" (428). She raises the readers' awareness of the fact that the real person who writes the book may be quite different from the implied author.

Through her occult Automatic Writing and by 'entering the mirror', Joan has moved "beyond the mirror of her texts", i.e. "beyond the conventionalised signs that cover up her repressed experience" (Staels 100). This becomes clear when we focus on the results of Joan's Automatic Writing and discuss what it reveals about herself (*LO* 268-9):

Who is the one standing in the prow
Who is the one voyaging
under the sky's arch, under the earth's arch
under the arch of arrows
in the death boat, why does she sing

She kneels, she is bent down
under the power
her tears are dark
her tears are jagged
her tears are the death you fear
Under the water, under the water sky
her tears fall, they are dark flowers

Joan says she "wasn't at all sure what this meant" (*LO* 269), and she wonders what Arthur was going to think about it, "this unhappy but torrid and ... slightly preposterous love affair between a woman in a boat and a man in a cloak, with icicle teeth and eyes of fire?" (*LO* 274). Joan already fears that a link between this book and her real life might be established. In fact, Arthur suspects that the work is about him and Joan's dissatisfaction with their marriage, so he does not approve of his wife's success. Bearing in mind that the product of Joan's first attempt at automatic writing is "a single long red line that twisted and turned back on itself, like a worm or a snarl of wool" (*LO* 134f), which is an image recalling a maze (or rather a person trying to get out of it with the help of "a snarl of wool"), we see how the products of Automatic Writing give an inside view into Joan's mind and her own repressed past. Further evidence for this is that Joan considers her poems to be subversions of Gothic formulas:

> On rereading, the book seemed quite peculiar. In fact, except for the diction, it seemed a lot like one of my standard Costume Gothics, but a Gothic gone wrong. It was upside-down somehow. There were the sufferings, the hero in the mask of a villain, the villain in the mask of a hero, the flights, the looming death, the sense of being imprisoned, but there was no happy ending, no true love. The recognition of this half-likeness made me uncomfortable. Perhaps I should have taken it to a psychiatrist instead of a publisher [… but] no one would understand about the Automatic Writing. (*LO* 282)

She already suspects that her 'true' past and 'real' life have written themselves into these poems, which raises her awareness of a reality beyond (or above?) her constructed fantasy.

There are several hints which assist the reader's interpretation of Joan's poem: the image of a woman in a death boat, singing her last song, is an intertextual reference to Tennyson's "The Lady of Shalott"[101]. The title for Joan's book, as chosen by the publishers Morton and Sturgess, their emphasis that her work resembles a combination of Khalil Gibran[102] and Rod McKuen[103], and the jacket blurb[104] are further hints, inasmuch as they reveal that individual readers may decode different meanings.

Joan explicitly hints at what she fears has written itself into her poems, for earlier in the novel she has expressed her insecurities about being powerful enough to try the Automatic Writing: "I wasn't sure I wanted great powers. What if I failed, enormously and publicly? What if no messages would come? It was easier not to try" (*LO* 132). She fears that she might be utterly hollow inside so that there is no message to be interpreted.

Howells points to a significant characteristic of an oracle when she says that "it is a voice which comes out of a woman's body and is associated with hidden

---

[101] The significance of this intertext, which permeates the whole narrative, is analysed in chapter 6.5.4.

[102] Khalil Gibran (1883-1931) was a poet, philosopher, and painter, and a Lebanese immigrant to the United States. His best known work is *The Prophet* (1923), a book of 26 philosophical essays focusing on themes such as love, death, marriage, friendship, work, or freedom.

[103] *chansonnier* (or singer-songwriter) and "one of the revered poets of the late 60s love generation" (Muze UK Ltd, Encyclopaedia of Popular Music <http://www.theiceberg.com/artist/24772/rod_mckuen, 2002>.)

[104] The jacket blurb of "LO" says: "Modern love and the sexual battle, dissected with a cutting edge and shocking honesty" (*LO* 283); Joan does not think "the book was about that, exactly; but Sturgess assured [her] he knew what he was doing" (*LO* 283). It shows how a critical audience, whose main aim is a successful marketing of the book, interprets the poems.

dangerous knowledge, but [...] it is not her own voice" (67)[105]. If Joan is to be understood as an oracle, who in a trance-like state produces a coded message, then who is the voice speaking through her? This will be answered by a close look at the section from which the publishers have taken the title "Lady Oracle" (Section Five of Joan's manuscript, *LO* 274):

> She sits on the iron throne
> She is one and three
> The dark lady   the redgold lady
> the blank lady   oracle
> of blood, she who must be
> obeyed   forever
> Her glass wings are gone
> She floats down the river
> singing her last song

The Lady Oracle is "one and three," which means that she is one person but made up of three different identities. This leads to the conclusion that Joan has written a poem about the Triple Goddess. Staels argues that "the dark lady" symbolises "the cold, repressive ice-goddess Hecate; the redgold lady or Diana, the maiden who is capable of freedom; the blank lady oracle of blood or Venus, source of love and life energy" (99).

According to Howells, this piece "both veils and reveals Joan's repressed memories of her mother" (74). Most importantly, however, it reveals the repressed shadow fragments of Joan's past and personality. During her experiments with Automatic Writing Joan feels a dark shadow figure standing behind her. After her mother's death Joan repeatedly dreams about her "three-headed mother, menacing and cold"[106] (*LO* 258). After the appearance of her mother's astral body in Terremoto, Joan eventually identifies her mother as her muse:

> It had been she standing behind me in the mirror, she was the one who was waiting around each turn, her voice whispered the turns [...]. She needed her freedom also; she had been my reflection too long [...]. My mother was a

---

[105] In their respective analyses Howells and Patton reveal that Atwood's research materials for *LO* consist mainly of information on oracles. The voice of the Delphic Oracle was the voice of Apollo, and earlier of the Earth Goddess (Patton 40f). Patton argues that in *LO* Atwood attempts to "re-imagine the Delphic oracle again under the control of women" (41); however, Atwood tends to favour equally-balanced power-politics and maybe only wants to raise an awareness of the difficulties women artists encounter in a patriarchal (literary) society.

[106] Staels argues that "Joan enlarges her mother to a cold Hecate figure, a hard, all-powerful death-goddess" (92).

vortex, a dark vacuum, I would never be able to make her happy. Or anyone else. Maybe it was time for me to stop trying. (*LO* 399f)

It is therefore Joan's mother, who reveals to her daughter the shadowy aspects of her own personality, which Joan has repressed for too long and which have manifested themselves in the ghost of her mother. Joan realises that she is not a Victorian paragon of true femininity, i.e. "patient and forbearing, warm, a sympathetic listener" and that she, too, can hurt people by becoming "mean and irritable" (*LO* 257). Joan comes to terms with her past, which symbolises a reconciliation with her repressed Diana identity; therefore, she can also forgive her mother, as Hecate "is not sinister when viewed as part of a process [...] but she does become sinister when she is seen as the only alternative, as the whole of the range of possibilities for being female" (*Survival* 199). By accepting her multi-fold personality, including her past and present, Joan can eventually forgive her mother and overcome her fear of "the dark lady .../ ...oracle/ ... who must be/ obeyed".

Significantly, Joan remembers explaining to Arthur that the mother she invented "for his benefit" died of "a rare disease – *lupus*[107] I think it was – shortly after I met him" (*LO* 43). This not only calls to mind werewolf stories and the Grimm's fairy tale of *Little Red Riding Hood*, who is threatened by a villainous wolf, just like Joan perceives herself as being threatened by her mother. It also reminds us of the philosophical saying *homo homini lupus*[108].

The proverb was coined by the Roman writer Plautus (?-184 BC). The (radical) rationalist Thomas Hobbes (1588-1679), a contemporary of René Descartes, later used it in his *De cive, Epistola dedicatoria*. As Hobbes' theories were very influential in their time and are still recognised nowadays, the saying was widely popularised and as a result tends to be attributed to him rather than to Plautus. The statement expresses that human beings treat each other like wolves, for they themselves are their worst enemy. In his famous work *Leviathan* (1651) Hobbes deduces the reason for absolute monarchy from this philosophical assumption, as in any other form of (constitutional) government all human beings would constantly be at war with each other[109].

---

[107] Lat. 'wolf'; tubercular skin disease
[108] Lat. 'Man is a wolf to man'
[109] see Audi, *The Cambridge Dictionary of Philosophy*

While Atwood certainly does not want to proclaim any such radical philosophy, she does express that human beings are duplicitous, and that we contain our own wolf. Once Joan accepts that she is capable of hurting people, too, i.e. that she can be "a duplicitous monster", she can also forgive her mother and end "the war" which "was on in earnest" between them in her childhood (*LO* 110).

6.1.4. The Triple Goddess

The Triple Goddess assumes a central position in *LO*[110] for she is impersonated and parodied by the artist Joan Foster to discuss the nature of artistic creation and the relationship between the woman artist and society. According to Patton, Atwood emphasises two aspects of the Goddess: "the most terrifying aspect [...], the devouring, cannibalistic Venus who mates with men and eats them [...] and her role as silent muse" (31-2). Eventually, Joan embodies all three identities: Diana, Venus, and Hecate[111]. Even though starting out as silent muse, Joan becomes audible in the end.

When the Polish Count tells Joan "in moments of contemplative passion" that she has "the body of a goddess", Joan finds this compliment rather "ambiguous" (*LO* 169), especially because "some goddesses didn't have bodies at all; there was one in the museum, three heads on top of a pillar, like a fire hydrant" (*LO* 169). Likewise, after her first sexual encounter with the Royal Porcupine and his remark that her "ass" is nice but not really different from anybody else's, she angrily considers he might have expected "three buttocks" and "nine tits" (*LO* 297). Both men do not value her writing: Paul feels envious when she begins to earn more money than he does – Joan can touch-type her romances and thus produce them faster –, and the Royal Porcupine considers her "a successful bad writer" (*LO* 290). They cast her in the role of the Triple Goddess as silent muse which Joan rejects as much as that of a self-destructive woman artist.

In Terremoto Joan remembers that after the publication of the "LO" poems she felt the need to escape with Arthur for a while. During their holiday in Italy they went

---

[110] Patton points out that "Atwood's research materials for the novel consist primarily of photocopied articles and references to the Goddess and to the Sybil" (32).
[111] The Hecate identity is represented by her mother. Joan eventually accepts her mother as a part of herself and thus embodies all three identities.

to the enormous maze in the Villa d'Este (near Rome) to look at the famous water-work statues[112], she saw sphinxes, "water shooting from their nipples" and the many-breasted Earth-Goddess Diana of Ephesus:

She had a serene face, perched on top of a body shaped like a mound of grapes. She was draped in breasts from neck to ankle, as though afflicted with a case of yaws: little breasts at the top and bottom, big ones around the middle. The nipples were equipped with spouts, but several of the breasts were out of order. I stood licking my ice-cream cone, watching the goddess coldly. Once I would have seen her as an image of myself, but not any more. My ability to give was limited, I was not inexhaustible. [...] I wanted things, for myself. (*LO* 308)

"Diana of Ephesus," *Windows to the Universe*, UCAR 2004
<http://www.windows.ucar.edu/tour/link=/mythology/images/diana_garden_jpg_image.html>.

Patton argues that

> like the Goddess who offers her breasts, her substance, for public consumption, the poet offers herself, her ideas, her selves, and her fears for public consumption. Her novels or poems will be "condensed", "digested" by reviewers, "consumed" by the public, "devoured" by fans, "regurgitated" in literature classes – she will be metaphorically cannibalized. (Patton 44)

Atwood parodies and trivialises the Goddess when she plays with the image of a malfunctioning Earth Goddess, who is gazed at by people licking ice-creams. The Goddess seems out of place in contemporary society. As a goddess who is defined by the essential characteristic of "nourishment", society both captivates and exploits her. Joan knows this: "I didn't want to spend the rest of my life in a cage, as a fat whore, a captive Earth Mother for whom somebody else collected the admission tickets" (*LO*

---

[112] Self-reflexive Joan might be deceived by her memory, as she is careful to point out to the reader: "Had it happened or was I making it up? Had we really walked through the maze of Roman streets together ..." (*LO* 158).

398). And yet, as Patton points out, Atwood stresses also the oracular powers of the Goddess, "the force of her language" (46), for in her "Automatic Writing" séances Joan acts like an oracle and not as a silent muse.

6.2. Reconstructing One's Past: An Overlapping of Art and Life

> How reliable is memory ... – our individual memory, or our collective memory as a society?[113]

In *LO* Joan Foster attempts to reconstruct the events of her life by transforming them into the same neat narrative structure that mark all her Costume Gothics. When she says: "All my life I'd been hooked on plots" (*LO* 377), she asserts that her life has been determined by the literary tradition of the 19th century. Unfortunately, her desire for a happy ending of her-story, equivalent to the neat endings in her Costume Gothics, remains an illusion. Even when she is in Italy, where she attempts to cut off her ties to her former life, Joan still waits for Arthur to come and rescue her. When she assaults a reporter with her Cinzano bottle (*LO* 282), Joan explains: "I didn't really mean to hit him [...]. I mean, I meant to hit someone, but it wasn't personal, I'd never seen him before in my life, he was a complete stranger" (*LO* 417).

Joan is determined to start a new life but realises that she cannot let go of her old one, especially because she escaped to the place where Arthur and she were on holiday the year before, which constantly reminds her of him. As the narrator of her-story, she makes clear at the very beginning that her account is retrospective. She attempted to leave behind "the shadow of a corpse, a shadow everyone would mistake for solid reality" and says: "At first I thought to have managed it" (*LO* 3). She anticipates that her scheme to feign her own death by drowning will not be successful, which leads Clara Thomas to conclude that "the subsequent story that we read must be substantially the same as the one that Joan told the reporter who found her after she made her final, panic-stricken bid for freedom and an indulgence that would relieve her from living with her past's reality" (161-2). Readers, however, do not have access to her oral tale, i.e. the story she recounts to the reporter. They only have the text version presumably written down by him.

---

[113] *In Search of* Alias Grace 9

Joan also makes clear that she is a rather unreliable narrator: "I talked too much, of course, but I was feeling nervous. I guess it will make a pretty weird story once he's written it; and the odd thing is that I didn't tell any lies. Well, not very many. Some of the names and a few other things, but nothing major" (*LO* 417). She is a growingly unreliable narrator but also honest (towards the reader) about her lies to other characters within the novel. Throughout her account Joan tries to justify the lies and constructions of her fictitious selves: "This was the reason I fabricated my life, time after time: the truth was not convincing" (*LO* 180). As regards Arthur, Joan is sure to have constructed her fictitious past "for his benefit" and she even "included a few items of truth" (*LO* 207). Even if she herself is aware of and honest about her lies, from a psychoanalytical point of view[114] memory only "functions like a muse creating fictive pasts" and thus the process of self-discovery is "rather a process of self-creation" and therefore an overlapping of art and life or an anti-mimetic attitude (Schier 3).

Joan is a self-reflexive narrator who reflects upon her own writings as artifice[115]. She discusses the writing process when composing her Costume Gothics and poetry and also their reception. Even though Joan assumes no responsibility for what she writes, "she tells us a great deal about herself – her fears and ambitions and her forbidden feelings" (Howells 69). Lecker believes that the first person narrator is the reporter to whom Joan has recounted her tale, i.e. that he is the "*ghost writer*" who tells the story (194): "Although the first person voice which speaks in *Lady Oracle* seems to be Joan Foster's it isn't hers at all. The story is told – with eminent appropriateness – by a *ghost writer* whose creation provides a metaphorical and ironic commentary on Joan's inability to tell the tale which would give form to her shifting sense of self" (194). It is likely that the reporter has at least 'edited' Joan's account for she says: "I guess it will make a pretty weird story once he's written it" (*LO* 417). As so often in Atwood's novels it is revealed only at the very end that the woman narrator has no authority over her own story, and that the account has already been interpreted by someone else.

---

[114] "The notion of identity as achieved by memory becomes questionable by the Freudian discovery that subconscious mechanisms colour, even falsify the memory of past experiences" (Schier 3).
[115] However, the metafictional quality of *LO* is achieved through parody rather than the self-reflexive narrator Joan Foster. She does not explicitly discuss the (seeming) dichotomy between reality and art, but she implicitly questions unmediated reference to the external world as she perceives reality through the fantasy world of her Costume Gothics – in a very exaggerated, parodic manner.

The retrospective account of Joan Foster's life resembles a labyrinth or a distorting mirror maze similar to the maze Charlotte eventually enters in *Stalked by Love*. In reconstructing her life Joan is "lost in her own funhouse"[116]: "For Arthur there were true paths, several of them perhaps, but only one at a time. For me there were no paths at all. Thickets, ditches, ponds, labyrinths, morasses, but no paths" (*LO* 203). Joan identifies with her heroine Charlotte, who in *Stalked by Love* "felt drawn towards the maze, irresistibly, against her will, yet she knew that if she went in, something terrible would happen to her" (*LO* 225). Joan fears the revelation of the truth about herself but she also knows that she "would have to go into the maze, there was no way out of it" (*LO* 402).

Joan Foster prefers to escape from reality and is aware that she is fabricating her life. She sees reality through the distorting mirror of her Costume Gothics and other popular art conventions. Her vision of herself depends on the perspective of her mother, the other and on the male gaze in particular. Telling her fragmentary story is her first attempt at coming to terms with her past and in so doing, locating herself in the present.

6.3. Joan Foster: "Escape Artist"

In Italy, her refuge, Joan realises that she has repeatedly run away from the interaction with others in her life: "I was an artist, an escape artist. I'd sometimes talked about love and commitment, but the real romance of my life was that between Houdini and his ropes and locked trunk; entering the embrace of bondage, slithering out again. What else had I ever done?" (*LO* 405). She knows about her tendency to escape and lead a passive existence, and considers herself a fated victim. At one point in the story Joan realises that she cannot live with the Royal Porcupine: "For him reality and fantasy were the same thing, which meant that for him there was no reality. But for me it would mean there was no fantasy, and therefore no escape" (*LO* 329). Joan's main problem results from attempts at self-deception as she has constructed a whole series of fictive identities for herself.

---

[116] "Lost in the Funhouse" is the title of John Barth's famous short story (published in 1968 in the short story collection *Lost in the Funhouse*), in which he metafictionally discusses the writing process.

In *Second Words* Atwood discusses the poem "Houdini" composed by the Canadian writer Eli Mandell (59f). She states that the poem is a direct reference to Marshall McLuhan, "trying desperately to get out of the realm of words, words, words, like the escape artist Houdini, for whom 'manacles, cells, handcuffs' were words, and who struggles to free himself from 'those binding words, wrapped around him/ like that mannered style, his formal suit'" (59). Joan, like the artist Houdini, is trapped in language as she reconstructs her past in 'escapist' or fictionalised versions of her life instead of actively assuming responsibility for her-story: "All my life I'd been hooked on plots", she resigns (*LO* 377). She needs to escape from real-life to repress her inner emptiness and imagine herself whole, as she is captivated by the illusion of a fixed and final meaning and the idea of a unified self.

Staels argues that Joan's role "remains that of a 'patient' or helpless victim from beginning to end" (81). While it is true that Joan has been determined to follow "the line of least resistance" in her life (*LO* 3), she does combat her victim role in the end. Moreover, she is determined to continue writing popular literature: "I won't write any more Costume Gothics, though; I think they were bad for me. But maybe I'll try some science fiction" (*LO* 418). Freibert argues this ending reveals that Joan will not remain in the victim position any longer:

> Joan decides that she will write no more gothics but will turn to science fiction. The gothics are somewhat passive and are based on hope. Science fiction, on the contrary, is active. Based on vision and invention, it can make things happen [...]. Through the metaphor of Joan's life, Atwood suggests that women must begin to imagine themselves capable of doing and being whatever they would like. They must no longer look into the mirrors which society holds up to them as reality. (31)

It remains arguable if *popular* science fiction is less formulaic than popular romances; however, by telling her-story to the reporter Joan has started to combat the victim position. On the other hand, Joan might run the risk of falling back into her old life as she starts to nurse the hospitalised reporter and confesses that: "There is something about a man in a bandage" (*LO* 419). Joan has realised the necessity to end her career as escape artist; whether she will be strong enough to do so in the future, however, is left open.

6.4. Intratextuality and the Merging of Fiction and Reality

In *LO* Joan's perception of reality is mediated through the fantasy worlds of her Costume Gothics. The boundaries between her popular romances and reality blur repeatedly, until they merge in the end. I will discuss an exemplary passage where reality and fiction coincide, before I focus on the climactic ending in more detail.

At times Joan literally steps from fantasy into real world, for example when she runs into Arthur. In Hyde Park Joan is walking the route about to be taken by her fictional heroine Samantha Deane, who must flee from the advances of an aristocratic villain. At the very point of Joan's rehearsal when the heroine is about to be assaulted and touched on her arm, Joan's own arm is touched by Arthur. Screaming of fear, Joan realises she has hit the supposed villain to the ground and (slightly) hurt his cheek, so that it is Joan herself who ironically becomes the "assailant" (*LO* 197). With Arthur and his banning-the-bomb pamphlets Joan believes to have found "a melancholy fighter for almost lost causes, idealistic and doomed, sort of like Lord Byron, whose biography I had just been skimming" (*LO* 198). She remarks that "unfortunately, he was only a Canadian like me, but I overlooked this defect" (*LO* 198). This passage shows that Joan tends to be so lost in her imagination that it affects her perception of reality: she sees reality through the lens of her popular romances.

Fiction and reality merge completely when Joan is in Terremoto, trying hard to finish the composition of the Costume Gothic *Stalked by Love* because of financial reasons: "I'd never be finished with Charlotte at the rate I was going, and my own financial future depended on hers" (*LO* 156). Joan, who has just staged her own death in hope of a "neat ending" (*LO* 357), decides that Charlotte's antagonist, "Felicia, [...] would have to die; such was the fate of wives" so that "Charlotte would then be free to become a wife in her turn" (*LO* 383). By killing Felicia, Joan hopes to provide a happy life for Charlotte.

Unfortunately, "Felicia was still alive and [Joan] couldn't seem to get rid of her" (*LO* 384), just like she couldn't seem to get rid of her former selves: "Below me, in the foundations of the house, I could hear the clothes I'd buried there growing themselves a body [...] It was the Fat Lady" (*LO* 388). She is still haunted by her image as a fat child and – even worse – her landlord brings her the wet clothes she had 'buried', and reveals that the villagers have all recognised her as the Joan Foster who had been there with her husband Arthur the year before. Joan has failed in staging a neat ending and thereby bringing her life to a neat closure because it turns out not to have been "terminal" (*LO* 357). Her attempt to vanish and re-emerge as someone else is not successful this time. Likewise, she seems unable to get rid of Felicia. Joan lets her drown in an unfortunate accident when, against all odds, Felicia returns in the shape of "an enormously fat woman" (*LO* 390). In her attempt to make it up with Redmond, Felicia starts to call him "Arthur". At precisely the moment when Redmond asks puzzled: "Who is Arthur?", Felicia begins to fade away again (*LO* 391).

Joan pictures Felicia in such a way that she becomes her mirror image: both have long "flame-red" hair, green eyes, and small white teeth (*LO* 37; 162). When Felicia looks into her mirror, she sees what Joan feels deep inside: "[…] there were flames, there was water, she was gazing up at herself from beneath the surface of a river. She was afraid of death. All she wanted was happiness with the man she loved. It was this impossible one wish that had ruined her life; she ought to have settled for contentment, for the usual lies" (*LO* 387). Immediately after writing these words, Joan notices the subversion of the conventional formula of her Costume Gothics: "Sympathy for Felicia was out of the question, it was against the rules, it would foul up the plot completely" (*LO* 387). Joan has problems finishing the narrative for Felicia refuses to conform to her conventional role, and Charlotte seems too pure to be real:

> I was getting tired of Charlotte, with her intact virtue and her tidy ways. Wearing her was like wearing a hair shirt, she made me itchy, I wanted her to fall into a mud puddle, have menstrual cramps, sweat, burp, fart. Even her terrors were too pure, her faceless murderers, her corridors, her mazes, and forbidden doors […]. Maybe I should try to write a real novel, about someone who worked in an office and had tawdry, unsatisfying affairs. But that was impossible, it was against my nature. I longed for happy endings. (*LO* 387)

Like her products of the Automatic Writing séances, this narrative seems to become another "Gothic gone wrong" and to turn into Joan's autobiography (*LO* 282). Joan identifies with Felicia, a woman who has to be sacrificed to save the all too pure Charlotte, a Victorian paragon of true femininity. Finding herself in sympathy with Felicia and bored by Charlotte, she decides to let them enter the maze. Grace points out that

> in classical myth the maze is closely associated with oracles and rites of rebirth or transformation from one state to another [...] they were originally intended as tests, either in the tactical defence of a fort, or at the entrance of sacred places, especially caves. Their double purpose was either to exclude the undesirable or provide ingress for the ally or initiate. [...] Upon reaching the centre of the maze, the initiate finds the desired wisdom or rebirth [...]. (1980:120)

In *Stalked by Love* the housekeeper tells Charlotte that Redmond's first two wives were lost in the maze. Lady Felicia, his third wife, "knew the maze was dangerous, but this very fact excited her. [...] She felt drawn towards the maze, irresistibly, against her will, yet she knew that if she went in, something terrible would happen to her" (*LO* 385). Joan/Felicia, curious wife of a Bluebeard-husband, feels drawn towards the maze but also fears the revelation about her inner self.

When Joan/Felicia reaches the centre of the maze, "she suddenly [finds] herself in the central plot" (*LO* 413), i.e. both in the centre of Bluebeard-Redmond's garden and her own story. In the penultimate chapter of *LO* "the merging of the frames is complete" (Kolodny 94). Joan/Felicia is confronted by four women, who symbolise the female images Joan used to identify with in her life and who she desperately tried to keep apart: two women have red hair, green eyes, and small white teeth (Joan/Felicia), one resembles her Aunt Lou (Louisa K. Delacourt), and the last is The Fat Lady from the Freak Side Show (symbolising her repressed childhood). They introduce themselves as "Lady Redmond" and say: "Every man has more than one wife. Sometimes all at once, sometimes one at a time, sometimes one he doesn't even know about" (*LO* 414). Through the confrontation with her discarded selves, Joan realises that her identity is complex and multi-fold, i.e. that she is "one and three", a multiplicity with unity.

At first Joan/Felicia considers staying inside the maze, where she is safe, but then she decides to open the door (representing the entrance to reality) and face her Bluebeard-husband, the murderous villain Redmond. Redmond is successively transformed into the various men in Joan's life and Redmond/Arthur eventually offers to rescue Joan/Felicia. This is when Joan realises that she has to combat her victim position. At precisely the moment when Redmond/Arthur is trying to kill Joan/Felicia, Joan hears footsteps on the gravel path in front of her apartment and decides: "I would have to face the man who stood waiting for me, for my life" (*LO* 416). She is determined to face and resist Bluebeard patriarchy, which 'amputates' women and women artists. Deciding not to take on the role of female-victim any longer, she takes an empty Cinzano bottle and assaults the 'murderous villain', who turns out to be a reporter who tracked her from Canada looking for a scandalous story and who is completely unknown to her.

In this instance of merging of the two narrative layers the Bluebeard theme is introduced as "a comic point of reference" (Bronfen 419). Joan does not identify with the heroines of fairy tales but with the fated victims. She feels "like Cinderella's ugly sister" (*LO* 310), and comments: "in a fairy tale I would be one of the two stupid sisters who open the forbidden door and are shocked by the murdered wives, not the third, clever one who keeps to the essentials: presence of mind, foresight, the telling of watertight lies. I told lies but they were not watertight" (*LO* 182). Eventually, however, she does take on the role of the third sister, who opens the door and faces the restraints imposed on women artists in a patriarchal society; patriarchy is symbolised by the 'murderous villain'.

According to Grace, *LO* shows that "we are Bluebeard, wife, and castle, repeating the story of our destruction, continuing to think in terms of hostile dualities, reducing our relationships with ourselves, each other, and the natural world to castles, to rooms with metal doors, to spaces separated from their context, exclusive and closed" (1984:260-1). By entering the maze, Joan undergoes a 'magical' transformation or rebirth and seems to have realised that her belief in miraculous rescues and escapes is the real danger in her life. Faced with her true self in the from of a multi-fold personality, including images the male gaze does not see, she is courageous enough to take her life in hand and tell her-story to the reporter. In doing so, she is able to re-enter life, and to go back to Canada. She has failed to complete her formulaic popular romance and started to take on responsibility for her own steps in the future. If she will continuously do so is left open.

6.5. Intertextual Relations in *Lady Oracle*

6.5.1. Introductory Remarks

In an interview by Struthers Atwood has mentioned several works that inspired her to write *LO*:

> *Northanger Abbey*, for sure. Part of Max Beerbohm's *A Christmas Garland* – the Gothic parts of the book are parodies of Gothic style. Further back, the popular form of Gothic descended – it's a corrupt form descending – from *Wuthering Heights*, on the one hand, along with *Jane Eyre* and *Pride and Prejudice*, I would say, on the other hand. (qtd. in Ljungberg 126)

The mentioning of *Northanger Abbey* and *A Christmas Garland* indicates the importance of parody in *LO*. Emily Brontë, in her 'unpopular'[117] Gothic romance *Wuthering Heights*[118], "acknowledged the existence of evil in the world without feeling the need to condemn the evil-doer," Heathcliff, that is (Barnard 119). The acknowledgement of evil in the world is also an important aspect in Atwood's fiction. While these works are sources rather than intertexts, the following analyses intertextual relations in *LO*, starting with the least intertextual intensity and concluding with remarks on the 'death of the author' Joan Foster.

6.5.2. Thomas Hardy's *Tess of the D'Urbervilles: A Pure Woman* and Double Codes of Morality

Like Tess in Hardy's novel[119], Joan longs to marry but feels she can only do so if her future husband "knows the truth about me and accepted me as I was, past and present" (*LO* 237)[120]. She worries that if he found out that she herself was "the fat

---

[117] It is "unpopular" in the sense that it cannot be compared to popular romances of the twentieth century. In its time it was shocking and therefore very unpopular, mainly because of "its harshness, its brutality", and "its unflinching look at subjects that were taboo to writers [in Victorian times]", i.e. an emphasis on sexual and wild emotions (Barnard 118). The novel's unpopularity also resulted from the fact that it was "met with incomprehension" (Martin 424).
[118] It was first published in 1847 under the pseudonym Ellis Bell and is her only novel.
[119] first published in 1891
[120] This reference has also been mentioned by Bronfen (417); who does not analyse the intertextual relationship between Hardy's and Atwood's novel.

lady in the picture", he would find her "unethical", be "disgusted" and maybe even leave her (*LO* 237). She is about to tell him the truth about her past when Arthur interrupts her to say he already knows that she was living with another man when they met. Pleased that Arthur was curious enough to spy on her, Joan decides "to postpone [her] revelations to some later date" (*LO* 239), contrary to Hardy's Tess.

Joan and Tess are both 'pure' women in the sense that they are 'faultless'; they suffer from societal restrictions and expectations of women and are subject to the 'male gaze'[121]. In Victorian times Tess would not have been considered a pure woman from the perspective of the dominant other, i.e. the 'male gaze'. Hardy aimed at a critical evaluation of Victorian society by laying bare the double codes of morality in his novel: Tess had to die so that "Justice" could be done (*Tess* 397). Joan feels she does not correspond to contemporary society's image of a woman and a woman artist, so she aims to re-construct this image by telling her-story, and in doing so, be able to go back to Canada. She tries to justify her self-denial in the past, which resulted from seeing herself as seen by the (m)other and patriarchal other. While Hardy wrote his novel to comment on Victorian society, Atwood uses the (parodic) intertextual reference to comment on contemporary society and question the double codes of morality regarding male and female artists.

6.5.3. Samuel Taylor Coleridge's "The Rime of the Ancient Mariner"

Throughout *LO* there are repeated intertextual references to Samuel Taylor Coleridge's "The Rime of the Ancient Mariner" (1798). Fee points out that the poem's function is to mirror the problems of articulation and survival in the novel (50). In Coleridge's ballad, the Mariner fixes his audience, an innocent wedding-guest on his way to a wedding, with his "glittering eye" to tell his story (l. 3) of how he once shot an innocent albatross in an act of mere cruelty, an act that cut him off "from the healing, restorative, natural world" (Barnard 95). He was punished by having to carry the dead bird around his neck and doomed to live a "Life-in-Death", a life in limbo. Through admiration of the natural world, symbolised by the beauty of water-snakes in the moonlight, he could re-unite with nature, and the albatross fell

---

[121] Selden et al. point out that the character Tess "is often regarded as composed of images set up by the male gaze she is constantly subject to" (157).

from his neck. Given back his voice, he is now forced to tell his tale of guilt and suffering over and over again.

Joan's albatross is her guilt, symbolised by the haunting image of her mother. Joan feels that she failed to make her mother happy; thus, throughout her double life she has "carried [her] mother around [her] neck like a rotting albatross" (*LO* 258); however, she eventually realises: "I would never be able to make her happy. Or anyone else. Maybe it was time for me to stop trying" (*LO* 399-400). Once Joan accepts her multiple selves, which may not always correspond to restricting societal expectations of a woman, she can also forgive her mother.

Both the Mariner and Joan live in limbo: Joan is officially pronounced dead, but still alive on "the Other Side" of the Atlantic Ocean:

> The Other Side was no paradise, it was only a limbo. Now I knew why the dead came back to watch over the living: the Other Side was boring. There was no one to talk to and nothing to do. [...] I was feeling marooned; the impulse to send out messages [...] grew every day. I am still alive. Stuck here, have not sighted a ship for days. Am tired of talking to the local flora and fauna and the ants. (*LO* 375-6)

Both the Mariner and Joan are isolated from human society and both are enforced to tell their tale to re-enter life. Joan confesses her past to the reporter whom she 'assaults' in Terremoto. Once he lies in hospital, he is a literal captive to her tale.

Joan knows it depends on whether she can make her story sound believable or not that she can go back to Canada. She believes "it will make a pretty weird story once he's written it; and the odd thing is that I didn't tell any lies. Well, not very many. Some of the names and a few other things, but nothing major" (*LO* 417). The wedding guest has been told a 'true' story by the Mariner. When he leaves, he has been transformed into "a sadder and a wiser man" (l. 624). It is up to the readers of *LO* how much of Joan's tale they want to believe. In *SW* Atwood says that

> all writers play Ancient Mariner at times to the reader's Wedding Guest, hoping that they are holding the reader with their glittering eye, at least long enough so [s]he'll turn the next page. The tale the Mariner tells is partly about himself, true, but it's partly about the Universe and partly about something the Wedding Guest needs to know; or at least, that's what the story tells us. (348)

Joan's memoir is partly about herself, partly about the Universe", i.e. about the relation between truth and lie/fact and fiction, and "about something we need to know", i.e. the perils of conventional modes of perception in our daily lives.

6.5.4. Alfred Lord Tennyson's "The Lady of Shalott": Reality as Construct, Sacrificial Maidens and "The Rapunzel Syndrome"

Some preliminary remarks on Tennyson's "best-known anthology piece" are required before we move into an analysis of its intertextual quality in *LO* (Barnard 124). The ballad was first published in 1832 and later in a revised from in 1842, but the plot remained basically the same[122]. Both versions are structured in four parts.

The first part of the poem establishes the setting: four grey walled towers are encircled by lilies and willows[123] on the island of Shalott, positioned in the middle of a river which has agriculture on either side and boats going by. The river and a road in the fields lead to "many-towered Camelot", the mythical city seating King Arthur's court. On the "silent" island and imprisoned in the tower lives the legendary Lady of Shalott, destined to spend her time sitting with her back to the window and weave a tapestry of the "shadows" of the outside world, which she sees reflected in a mirror hanging over her loom[124]. Part two reveals that if she stops weaving her "magic web" to look out of her window and down to the city of Camelot, a dreadful and yet unknown curse will come upon her. So, she lives in her seclusion, weaving day and night, only becoming "half-sick of shadows" when she perceives a lately wedded couple in her mirror. The third part brings about the climax: one day her mirror reflects the tantalising image of Sir Lancelot, "representing activity, the real world, sex" (Barnard 124); Lancelot is heading for Camelot and to Queen Guinevere, the "lady in his shield". The Lady's desire to look out of the window at real life and

---

[122] In his comparative analysis of the two versions of "The Lady of Shalott" Reinfandt argues that Tennyson aimed at an elimination of elements of Romanticism in the 1842 version: "Tennyson's revision of 'The Lady of Shalott' can be interpreted as an indicator of the movement from a poetics of Romanticism emphasizing processes of social differentiation towards a poetics of realism emphasizing aspects of interference between differentiated social spheres" (315).

[123] The lilies and willows foreshadow the Lady's death; the plants also stress that there is no life on the island and underline the artist's isolation from the world.

[124] Reinfandt explains that the mirror is "not a poetic device, but a realistic feature of a loom, allowing the weaver to see the results of her work" (311).

merge with Lancelot brings about the curse: the moment she turns from her artefact her woven cloth flies out of the window and the mirror breaks[125]. In the fourth and final section the Lady exhales her last breath of life as she floats down the stormy river to the city of Camelot. She has written her name around the prow of her boat and the inhabitants of Camelot look at her dead body in surprise and awe.

Reinfandt points out that in traditional Tennyson criticism "The Lady of Shalott" is regarded as "an allegorical treatment of the relationship between art and life" (311). The Lady of Shalott is associated with artistic creation: the Lady represents the artist, "removed from life even as she reflects it, who is killed by the touch of reality that she longs for" (Barnard 124), or, in other words, "the artist must remain detached from life, experiencing it only through the imagination; when the artist looks on life directly, his artistic talent dies" (Jensen 33). In line with these interpretations Jensen argues that Joan's crisis consists in being unable to disentangle the role she assumes in reality (wife of Arthur) and her role as author of Costume Gothics (Louisa K. Delacourt). While this is evident, I want to argue that the intertextual reference to "The Lady of Shalott" underlines the central concern of *LO* as both texts discuss the relationship between art and reality: whereas Tennyson's poem argues for a dichotomy art/reality, *LO* does quite the contrary.

Atwood uses Tennyson's probably best-known poem to establish communicativity between author and reader. Moreover, she does not simply rely on her readers' knowledge of the text, but even hints at an interpretation of Tennyson's poem for Joan explicitly reflects on the relationship between art and reality. She remembers that even as a child she wanted "castles and princesses, the Lady of Shalott floating down a winding river in a boat" and that she had looked up the meaning of *shalott* in the dictionary: "*shalot, kind of small onion*. The spelling was different but not different enough" (*LO* 170). An onion consists of various layers (or 'frames'). A shallot is like an onion. The spelling of shallot is "not different enough" from the Lady of Shalott, the artist or art in general. Thus, art equals layers or 'frames'. Metafiction argues against the principle of mimesis as there is no unmediated experience of external reality: "neither historical experiences nor literary

---

[125] By breaking the mirror, the Lady of Shalott discards "the 'art' side for the hard and bright 'life' side, where the 'art' side is doomed to die" (*Negotiating* 56). Atwood points out that in the late nineteenth- and early twentieth-century "the artist is to be self-effacing; he is to be hidden from view and he is to serve his calling" for "the God of High Art [...] requires human sacrifices" (*Negotiating* 77-80).

fiction are unmediated or unprocessed or non-linguistic" and thus "content [...] will never be discovered in a 'natural' unframed state" (Waugh 30-1; see chapter 2.3.3.4.). This underlines that there is ultimately no dichotomy reality/fiction: art provides the frame through which we perceive external reality.

This is taken to extremes in *LO*, when Joan enforces formulaic conventions of popular art onto her real life. The Lady of Shalott weaves an artefact from "the mirror's magic sights". Joan's artefacts (and her life) are a mixture of fantasy and reality and she even wants to conjure her art up into being: Joan wishes to have popular art conventions coincide with reality, especially because she tries to project stereotypical gender roles onto human beings.

Barnard also points to another interpretation: "We may see, in aspects of [the Lady's] fate, a comment on Victorian womanhood, elevated on to a pedestal, yet shut away from the hurly-burly of life which may both invigorate and destroy" (124). In line with Barnard's interpretation Staels summarises the ending of the ballad as such: "The only outcome to the Lady's sacrificial urge and unrequited love, to the unresolved clash between ideality (fulfilment of the romance plot) and reality, is madness or death" (86).

After her staged boat accident Joan hopes to have left behind "the shadow of a corpse [...] everyone would mistake for solid reality" (*LO* 3). Even though Joan plans her drowning scene carefully, she loses her balance and falls over board quite inelegantly. This is Atwood at her best parodying Tennyson's Lady of Shalott. Through Joan's staged boat accident Atwood parodies the suicide of "Victorian sacrificial maidens" such as Tennyson's Lady of Shalott, "whose only solution to unrequited love was a passionate love-death" (Staels 78).

Staels further argues that Joan's continuing imitation of the Lady comments on her desire to reiterate the traditional role designed for women [in Victorian times], a role embodied both in nineteenth-century 'high' literature and twentieth-century popular romances" (86). Just as "Tennyson's Lady of Shalott used to be a cult figure to Victorian women of the middle-class", Joan hopes to achieve cult status, too (Staels 86); however, when Joan gets a letter from Sam, who congratulates her on having become "a death cult" and tells her that "sales of *Lady Oracle* were booming" because "every necrophiliac in the country was rushing to buy a copy", her feelings change (*LO* 380):

> I'd been shoved into the ranks of those other unhappy ladies, scores of them apparently, who'd been killed by a surfeit of words. There I was, on the bottom of the death barge, where I'd once longed to be, my name on the prow, winding my name down the river. Several of the articles drew morals: you could sing and dance or you could be happy, but not both. Maybe they were right, you could stay in the tower for years, weaving away, looking in the mirror, but one glance out the window at real life and that was that. The curse, the doom. I began to feel that even though I hadn't committed suicide, perhaps I should have. They made it sound so plausible. (*LO* 381)

She realises that her initial urge "to have someone, anyone, say that [she] had a lovely face, even if [she] had to turn into a corpse in a barge-bottom first" has been fulfilled (*LO* 170f); however, what will be remembered is nothing more than "her name on the prow" for she has – as author of the "LO" poems – achieved legendary "death cult" status. Joan has to face the fact that the media constructed their own narrative from her staged drowning plot.

Joan identifies her role as artist with the image of the Lady of Shalott. But after the last apparition of her mother's astral body Joan identifies her mother with the Lady of Shalott, too:

> She had been the lady in the boat, the death barge, the tragic lady with flowing hair and stricken eyes, the lady in the tower. She couldn't stand the view from her window, life was her curse. [...] She needed her freedom also.
> (LO 399-10)

According to Maclean, "Joan and her mother are mirror images of each other; both are modern Ladies of Shalott. Whereas Joan's mother is a prisoner of reality, Joan is a prisoner of fantasy" (185). Being a war bride and forced to marry because pregnant, Joan's mother is determined to sacrifice all her energy for her family[126]. Joan draws parallels between her-story and that of her mother, because both were determined by broken illusions. When her mother's astral body appears to Joan in Terremoto she remarks: "I loved her but the glass was between us, I would have to go through it. [...] Together we would go down the corridor into the darkness. [...] The door was locked. I shook it and shook it until it came open" (*LO* 399). In order to understand each other they both have to leave their prison-houses. Both are Canadian Rapunzel

---

[126] Zimmermann argues that this is the reason why she cannot dispose of the time for any creative project (114).

figures trapped in their tower: they have "internalised the values of [contemporary] culture to such an extent that they become [their] prison" (*Survival* 209).

Wilson states that "internal and external societal strictures against uncontrolled female creativity constitute gender thorns and walls confining the female artist to a fairy-tale tower" (1993:19). Thus, women artists may suffer from the "Rapunzel Syndrome" and have to overcome the expectation that "the artist must be a kind of Rapunzel: separate and distant from the work – necessarily a closed entity – from audience, and from life, society, history, and the world" (Wilson 1993:19).

6.5.5. Reel World Versus Real World: The Hollywood Film *The Red Shoes* and Andersen's *The Little Mermaid*

> Woman and Writer are separate categories; but in any individual woman writer, they are inseparable.[127]

References to Hollywood films are used to characterise Joan's mother, Aunt Lou and especially Joan herself as they reveal the characters' internalised culture code. Joan, for example, violently rejects her mother's desire to have her transformed into a mirror image of a Hollywood movie star. Mrs Delacourt names her daughter after the famous actress Joan Crawford and hopes her daughter will live up to this image. Joan sarcastically remarks that Joan Crawford's "real name was Lucille LeSueur, which would have suited me much better. Lucy the Sweet" (*LO* 45). Joan Crawford is thin, beautiful, successful and thus an ideal role model in her mother's point of view; Joan, however, is not and this is "one of the many things for which [her] mother never quite forgave [her]" (*LO* 45).

Atwood exaggerates and parodies the influence of popular art conventions on the characters' lives to such an extent that Hill Rigney is led to define Joan's mother as "a Walt Disney version of evil" (64). Through parody Atwood attempts to raise the reader awareness of societal norms which restrict the lives of individual people, and especially of women artists. This will become clear when we analyse the intertextual reference to the film *The Red Shoes*.

---

[127] *SW* 195

Both the film version[128] of Hans Christian Andersen's fairy tale *The Red Shoes*[129] and his fairy tale *The Little Mermaid* are parables on the woman artist's dilemma as they express the impossibility of combining love and success. *LO* comments on the ideology set forth in these stories: the novel depicts "the professional woman who wants both to be loved as a woman and to be respected for her mind" (Jensen 29).

Joan is captivated by the Hollywood film *The Red Shoes*, in which the ballet dancer Victoria Page, impersonated by Moira Shearer, is torn between her career and her husband. Atwood has described her experience when seeing the film as a teenager as such:

> A whole generation of little girls were taken to see it as a special treat for their birthday parties. Moira Shearer was a famous dancer but alas, she fell in love with the orchestra conductor, who, for some reason totally obscure to me at the time, forbade her to dance after they got married. This prohibition made her very unhappy. She wanted the man, but she wanted to dance as well, and the conflict drove her to fling herself in front of a train. The message was clear. You could not have both your artistic career and the love of a good man as well, and if you tried, you would end up committing suicide. (*SW* 224; see also *Negotiating* 85, 114)

Joan identifies with the ballet dancer Victoria Page, impersonated by Moira Shearer, also because both have long red hair. She remembers that from early childhood she "wanted those things too, [...] to dance and be married to a handsome orchestra conductor, both at once [...]" (*LO* 93-4). The message of the film *The Red Shoes* corresponds to the one in Andersen's fairy tale *The Little Mermaid*[130]. Joan feels:

> Perhaps [...] I had no soul; I just drifted around singing vaguely, like the Little Mermaid in the Andersen fairy tale. In order to get a soul you had to suffer, you had to give something up; or was that to get legs and feet? I couldn't remember. She'd become a dancer, though, with no tongue[131]. Then there was Moira Shearer in *The Red Shoes*. Neither of them had been able to

---

[128] dir. by Michael Powell and Emeric Pressburger (1948)
[129] Andersen's tale is less about a woman artist than "about worldly vanity and pride, its consequent punishment, and Christian redemption" (Wilson 1993:123). Wilson, however, thinks that like Karen in the Andersen's tale, Joan "dances out of control, in her addiction to escapism and repressive relationships as well as to eating" (1993:126).
[130] To win the love of a prince, the Little Mermaid sacrifices her voice in order to get human legs. Unfortunately, she cannot captivate the prince's interest in her without her voice, he marries someone else, and she dies in despair.
[131] She has become a 'dancer' in a metaphorical sense: her feet hurt so much when she walks that it feels like dancing on knives.

please the handsome prince; both of them had died. I was doing fairly well by comparison. Their mistake had been to go public, whereas I did my dancing behind closed doors. (*LO* 262)

Joan concludes that she must conceal her past and profession. She believes that as long as she can keep her artistic activities secret, she will be able to live out both roles, i.e. that of artist and wife. Thus, she is forced to become an 'escape' artist and conform to societal norms.

Problems arise after the publication of "LO", which Joan publishes under the name Joan Foster, a name by which people know her in real life. Unable to combine her public image of the artist with the role of wife of Arthur, and because Fraser Buchanan might reveal her secret identities, Joan tries to escape and sacrifices her identity as noted authoress. Like the artists in the Hollywood film and in Andersen's tale, Joan 'dies'; however, her death is just another constructed plot. Once escaped to Terremoto, Joan decides: "From now on [...] I would dance for no one but myself" (*LO* 405). She twirls around in her apartment and right into the window's broken glass[132] on the floor, so that she cuts her feet, which start to bleed:

> The real red shoes, the feet punished for dancing. You could dance, or you could have the love of a good man. But you were afraid to dance, because you had this unnatural fear that if you danced they'd cut your feet off so you wouldn't be able to dance. Finally you overcame your fear and danced, and they cut your feet off. The good man went away too, because you wanted to dance. (*LO* 406)

Still feeling like a fated victim, Joan realises that she is trapped by society's expectations, even though she always preferred the escape: "How could I escape now, on my cut feet?" (*LO* 406). She begins to see that her role as escape artist has been unsuccessful. Unlike her 'reel' predecessor Victoria Page alias Moira Shearer, Joan survives and she even recounts her tale; however – and maybe because still trapped in a 1970s patriarchal society, she only tells her story to be written down by a male reporter.

According to Atwood, "there is some truth to the *Red Shoes* syndrome. It *is* more difficult for a woman writer in this society than for a male writer [...] because it has been made more difficult" (*SW* 226). She goes on to explain that women are still

---

[132] As the window is broken, Joan slowly starts to get an 'unmediated view' onto reality from her apartment in Terremoto.

expected to be morally better than men and that a creative and thus powerful woman is likely to be considered "a witch, a Medusa", or "a destructive, powerful, scary monster" (226). In Atwood's opinion, if a woman writer wanted to be good at anything, she would have to sacrifice her femininity; if she wanted to be female, she would have to have her tongue (or voice) removed, like the Little Mermaid (*SW* 225).

Wilson points to a general pattern in Atwood's fairy tale intertexts: "Beginning by dancing for others, and becoming passively frozen, amputated and cannibalized, Atwood's personae transform themselves, often through magical eating or touching or through ritual immersion in the natural world" (1993:xii). Joan experiences a fairy-tale transformation: by telling her own story, she is able to begin again, "unlimited in the space at the end of the novel" (Wilson 1993:11). Even though Joan assumes no responsibility for what she writes, and even though her written account is only a mediated version, Joan has started to take responsibility for her life and no longer secludes herself from society.

6.6. Concluding Remarks: "The Death of the Author" Joan Foster

> Death and femininity are culturally positioned as the two central enigmas of western discourse. They are used to represent that which is inexpressible, inscrutable, unmanageable, horrible; that which cannot be faced directly but must be controlled by virtue of social laws and art.[133]

In her professorial dissertation *Over Her Dead Body* Elisabeth Bronfen argues that the aesthetically pleasing (narrative and visual) representations of death in the form of the dead feminine body, can be read as symptoms of our culture for they are failed repressions of "our knowledge of the reality of death precisely because here death occurs *at* someone else's body [clearly marked as being other[134]] and *as* an image" (x-xi)[135]. This idea resounds when Joan says: "If Desdemona was fat who would care whether or not Othello strangled her? Why is it that the girls Nazis torture on the covers of the sleazier men's magazines are always good-looking?" (*LO* 56).

---

[133] Bronfen 181
[134] Bronfen is right to argue that "the feminine body is culturally constructed as the superlative site of alterity" (Bronfen xi).
[135] Her underlying assumption is that "if symptoms are failed repressions, representations are symptoms that visualise even as they conceal what is too dangerous to articulate openly but too fascinating to repress successfully" (Bronfen xi).

In her analysis of *LO* Bronfen states that "Atwood explicitly thematises the proximity of death to the production of fictions of the self and to issues of feminine authorship" and parodies "cultural conventions that link women, writing, and death" (415). Joan is continuously caught between a denial and a re-formation of her self as she is visible to others only in the guise of her various doubles. On a surface level Joan's choice between art and life seems to be an either-or choice, especially because she has problems combining both roles in her own life. She refuses reality (and being a wife rather than an artist), but chooses art and dies like her 'reel' predecessors Moira Shearer and The Little Mermaid, or her 'real' predecessors Silvia Plath and Anne Sexton, i.e. by committing suicide. However, her death is only 'staged', and thus another artefact.

Joan gets the idea for her 'death-plot' from a newspaper article about a woman who drowned in Lake Ontario and was officially pronounced dead even though her corpse was never found. Through her constructed death Joan attempts to design herself anew; however, she does not discard her old self – or rather selves – to give birth to any 'true' identity but she attempts to design an artefact, which should corresponds to formulaic popular art conventions. Her drowning plot is to give birth to a constructed new personality and it is thus that Joan attempts to turn art into life. Once escaped to Terremoto and sitting on the balcony, Joan has "visions of [herself] as a Mediterranean splendor, golden-brown" even though she is wrapped in towels so as not to get freckles and sunburnt (*LO* 4), which shows the extent to which art determines her notions of reality, and how she still wishes to be 'aesthetically pleasing'.

Right at the beginning of the narrative Joan says: "I planned my death carefully; unlike my life, which meandered along from one thing to another, despite my feeble attempts to control it. [...] The trick was to disappear without a trace, leaving behind me the shadow of a corpse, a shadow everyone would mistake for solid reality" (*LO* 3). Ironically, the local newspapers do mistake the "solid reality" for they suspect the author's suicide and talk of Joan's "morbid intensity", "doomed eyes", and her apparent "fits of depression" so that Joan becomes " a death cult" (*LO* 380). Now that the newspapers have pronounced her death, she begins to feel: "Even though I hadn't committed suicide, maybe I should have. They made it sound so plausible" (*LO* 381). Atwood notes that the actress Sarah Bernhardt, who had herself photographed lying in her own coffin, "knew exactly what she was doing [...]

because this was the image of a woman artist the public wanted and could understand: a sort of half-dead nun" (*Negotiating* 84).

Through Joan's constructed drowning plot Atwood parodies a culture in which authors – like the suicidal poets Plath and Sexton – have become cult figures: society's image of Joan Foster, noted authoress of the "LO" poems, is an image of 'The Death of the Artist as a Young Woman'[136]. Her life is "distorted and romanticized" and her work "then interpreted in the light of the distorted version" (*SW* 200). Atwood argues that "female writers in the twentieth century are seen not just as eccentric and unfeminine but as doomed. The temptation to act out the role of isolated or doomed female artist, either in one's life or through one's characters, is quite strong" (*SW* 226).

However, Joan eventually realises she must return from the dead and go back to Toronto to save her friends who have been imprisoned for alleged murder: "Why had I concocted this trashy and essentially melodramatic script, which might end by getting us all killed in earnest?" (*LO* 367-8). She finally takes responsibility for her actions in planning to get Sam and Marlene out of jail. She knows that she will have to sacrifice the image of her 'aesthetically pleasing' body in the death barge in order to live or, as Thomas points out, "Joan did not rid herself of her past by her faked suicide, but she did engage in the process of bringing herself to real life, as it were, through telling her story" (172). In the retrospective account of her own story she inscribes "her own dance over her socialized steps in the past" (Wilson 1933:120). Joan has told her story, but Atwood's readers have read only the revised – and maybe even "weird" (*LO* 417) – version as written down by the male reporter. What we hear in his account is that Joan Foster, a woman artist, wants the range of possibilities open to any male artist.

---

[136] versus *A Portrait of the Artist as a Young Man*

7. THE BLIND ASSASSIN

7.1. Introductory Remarks on Plot and Multi-Layered Structure

Was einmal wirklich war, bleibt ewig möglich.[137]

BA, first published in 2000, is a highly complex novel as regards themes, structure and narrative technique. One reviewer, Murphy, considers the novel "the most writerly[138]" of Atwood's texts. Atwood constructs fictitious characters with interfigural relations to historical characters and fictitious events with intertextual relations to historical 'facts' and places them in a historically authentic setting. Her novel is an a-chronological sequence of fragmentary and yet also self-contained episodes, and it includes and plays with various genres[139].

BA is about the two sisters Iris and Laura, who are the granddaughters of the founder of a button factory in Port Ticonderoga, Canada. Fifty years after Laura's alleged suicide, Iris illuminates their intertwined pasts and re-evaluates events that made her sister drive off a bridge at the age of 25, only "ten days after the war ended" (*BA* 1). At the beginning, Laura's death remains the central enigma in the text but the reconstruction of Iris's life slowly reveals reasons for the younger sister's tragic end. It also shows Iris's maturing process, in which she is confronting the sexual power-politics in society. By reconstructing her own individual her-story Iris creates for herself an independent female identity. Her memoir is thus not only an investigation of Laura's death but also an account of how she comes to terms with her own past. With her memoir Iris wants to explain her family's history to her granddaughter Sabrina. As the sole survivor and all alone – since all her family are dead and Sabrina is in India – Iris feels urged to explain the 'true' story to Sabrina. However, in the course of the novel Iris realises the futility of this task since "the living bird is not its labelled bones" (*BA* 395).

The novel begins with an excerpt from Iris's memoir, an excerpt from Laura's novel, and a series of newspaper articles, which proclaim the accidental death of

---

[137] Menasseh ben Israel (1604-57): Rabbi, printer and diplomat. He approached Oliver Cromwell with a petition for the resettlement of Jews in England.

[138] Roland Barthes' distinction between readerly (*lisible*) and writerly (*scriptible*) texts: readerly texts are to be understood as 'windows onto reality', whereas writerly texts call attention to their fictional status.

[139] The structure of the novel bears resemblance to *AG*, where the protagonist's memories and dreams are juxtaposed with 'official' documents, such as newspaper articles.

Laura, and the natural death of Richard Griffen, an aspiring politician and Iris's husband. The third newspaper article from 1975 claims that Iris's daughter Aimee died of a broken neck. Iris is the self-reflexive first person narrator of *BA*. In Greek mythology Iris, the Goddess of the Rainbow, is also a messenger of the gods. In *SW* Atwood uses the example of the four messengers in the Book of Job to discuss the relationship between 'eye-witness' and literary audience:

> The book of Job begins with a series of catastrophes, but for each there is a survivor. Story telling at it's most drastic is the story of the disaster which is the world; it is done by Job's messengers, whom God saved alive because someone had to tell the story. *I only am escaped to tell thee.* When a story, 'true' or not, begins like this, we must listen. (350)

It seems as if Iris had been spared to tell her story and it will be shown that she considers it her duty to note down past events, events which she 'eye-witnessed'. The beginning of the novel, i.e. a juxtaposition of personal notes and newspaper clippings, stresses that private memory is to be compared and contrasted with public memory throughout the novel.

In an online review of *BA* Clark pays attention to the fact that "Iris Chase Griffen, like the heroines of *Surfacing* and *Cat's Eye*, has embarked on a return journey to her past from the isolated outpost of the present" and that "unlike them, her voyage is not literal but literary". Throughout this literary voyage *BA* discusses the nature of art and the notion of absolute knowledge or truth. The novel is centrally concerned with the relationship between fiction and reality and public and private memory. *BA* discusses the construction of fiction and the representation of reality and by means of self-reflexivity and intertextuality the novel draws attention to its status as literary artefact[140].

Atwood's *BA* has a Chinese-box structure: a pulp (dystopian) science fiction novel is embedded in a confessional romance, which is nested in a memoir novel; in addition, there are local and national newspaper clippings and a medical letter, which all qualify the various threads of narration. The resulting narrative is a highly complex artefact, similar to that produced by the child carpet weavers who are mentioned in the science fiction story. The scrapbook-like novel also mirrors Iris's individualistic assessment of time and events as shaped by her memory. Her memoir

---

[140] The novel also discusses the social inequalities of the 1930s, themes of mortality and death, revenge, and the mother-daughter relationship, depicting both childhood and womanhood and giving the perspective of both mother and daughter.

moves from the present to past memories, includes dreams and Iris's reflections on her role as narrator of the 'true' story.

The outermost layer of the complex narrative is the memoir novel written by Iris Griffen, née Chase, who attempts to throw light on 20th –century Canadian history and the personal history of the Chase family. In her review, Brookner neatly summarises the main events in the Chase family: "Father returning shattered from France, Mother patiently resigned to his eccentricities, the family business […] first flourishing then undergoing decline, faithful housekeeper given to wise saws and modern instances, and a general air of threatened prosperity and social status" (50).

The main action in Iris's memoir takes place during the 1930s and 40s. In chronological flashbacks she recounts the lives of her grandparents and parents, stories she has been told mainly by the housekeeper Reenie and constructed herself by looking at Grandmother Adelia's scrapbook. Iris describes how her mother's frail health and especially her death had an effect on the relationship between the two sisters: Iris was to take on growing responsibility for her younger sister, who was thus becoming more and more a burden to her. She depicts significant historical events in the first half of the twentieth century, events which result first in the rise and then in the fall of the Chase industries. Iris's father literally sells her off into a marriage with Richard to save his factories and provide for his two daughters: in exchange for his daughters' economic security, Chase turns over the remains of his estate. Iris consents to marrying Richard, mainly because of the prospect of "nice clothes" and the hope to be relieved of the burden of Laura (*BA* 237). Before the marriage is arranged, the sisters meet Alex Thomas, a young communist, who on a Labour Day Picnic triggers their emotional and sexual maturing process. When the Chase factories burn down, he is accused of being the arsonist – most likely due to Richard's influence. Laura hides him with the help of Iris in their attic at Avilion; after he leaves the sisters, he is continuously on the run and both Laura and Iris seem to remain involved with him. The subtext in Iris's memoir depicts her own blindness to or ignorance of the events around her, events which have led to her sister's suicide.

Intertwined with these flashbacks is a novel which is also called *The Blind Assassin*[141], apparently written by Laura[142] and published posthumously in 1947, two years after her death. It is set in the 1930s and describes a love affair between a wealthy married woman in her early twenties (who the reading public presumes to be Laura) and a young communist in his mid thirties (presumed to be Alex Thomas), who is hiding from the police and trying to make a living by writing pulp science fiction stories. In their clandestine meetings the unnamed couple constructs the plot of a pulp science fiction novel, i.e. the story within Laura's novel and the innermost layer of Atwood's narrative, which parallels the two outer layers. It describes a class-conscious society, in which the wealthy and (thus) powerful exploit the weak. In this society on the planet Zycron, child carpet weavers, once blinded by the work, become prostitutes or are hired as assassins for they can cut throats in the dark; hence also the saying among these children that "only the blind are free" ("BA" 22):

> The carpets were woven by slaves who were invariably children, because only the fingers of children would be small enough for such intricate work But the incessant close labour demanded of these children caused them to go blind by the age of eight or nine, and their blindness was the measure by which the carpet sellers valued and extolled their merchandise: This carpet blinded ten children they would say. ("BA" 22)

This innermost layer, and in particular the themes of power-politics, mirror the story of the lovers by depicting the social gap between them and the sacrifices and betrayals connected with their affair; furthermore, both layers of Laura's novel parallel events described in Iris's fictional autobiography. Towards the end of *BA* Iris reveals to the reader that she is the author of and the unnamed woman in "BA"; however, the narrative is constructed in such a way that both of the sisters could be Alex's lover.

Interspersed with Iris's memoir and Laura's novel are newspaper clippings, i.e. society columns and death notices, and a letter written by the director of the Bella Vista sanctuary to which Richard has Laura confined to hide her pregnancy. These clippings, which advance the unfolding of the plot, are contrasted with Atwood's counter-narrative, i.e. they discuss socio-political events from an outside but not

---

[141] Hereafter referred to as "BA" in the text to facilitate a differentiation between the intertwined narratives.
[142] The novel is signed in her name but the true authorship is revealed in Iris's memoir. To facilitate differentiation I still refer to the embedded narrative as "Laura's novel".

necessarily objective point of view, as becomes clear through Iris's portrayal of events; furthermore, they emphasise the constructed, scrap-book-like quality of the narrative.

Through the inclusion of these clippings *BA* discusses the relationship between historical fact and experiential event, and between public and private memory. According to Brookner, the newspaper articles "put a polite gloss on the brute facts" (2). What appear to be facts at the beginning are given a different interpretation through Iris's memoir. The following chapters comment on the similarities and differences of these various forms in the novel and on how they help to form a composite picture of reality or truth.

7.1.1. Utopias, Dystopias, and Imagined Societies on the Planet Zycron

> A writer's job is to tell his society not how it ought to live, but how it does live.[143]

HT, set in an imaginary future, is commonly defined as a feminist dystopian novel[144]. Mahoney defines feminist dystopia as "the future fiction set in a 'bad place' for women [...], in which women can unravel and re-imagine existing power relations" (29). Both *HT* and "BA" deal with sexual power politics in a dystopian society. After the publication of *HT* Atwood pointed out in a CBC interview that "there isn't anything in the book that isn't based on something that hasn't already happened in history or in another country or for which the materials are not already available[145]" (qtd. in Kolodny 109). Her statement clarifies that this piece of speculative fiction mirrors historical and contemporary socio-politics.

The same is true for the story about the child carpet weavers in "BA", even though it is a pulp science fiction story written in the tradition of the 1930s dime novel. McCracken points out that "at the root of all science fiction lies the fantasy of

---

[143] *Survival* 42

[144] While exact definitions of dystopian novels may vary, *dystopia* is understood as the antonym of *eutopia* or *utopia*. Sir Thomas More derived the term *utopia* as a neologism (or even pun) from the Greek word *eutopos* ['good place'] and the general negative *ou-* [*outopos* meaning 'no place'] to form the title of his famous novel (Baldick 235). More's *Utopia* (1516) describes an imagined society of ideal perfection; dystopian novels, on the other hand, depict bad places with corrupt societies.

[145] *O&C* is another dystopian novel constructed of current materials.

alien encounter" (102). Science fiction as exemplified in the dime novel of the 1930s, takes place on other planets in another dimension of time. Atwood explains that this type of popular fiction "had bug-eyed monsters, it had lizard men, and the two-thousand-year-old-undead women have a long pedigree" (interview by Reynolds 20). She further notes that

> those works were also stuffed with colour adjectives. Partly because the pulps themselves were not illustrated in colour. They had colour covers, but that kind of printing hadn't been perfected yet, so inside they were black and white, and everything is therefore 'azure' or 'sapphirine' – all of these very exotic descriptions. (interview by Reynolds 21)

The use of colour adjectives – and also the absence of colour – is an important element which links "BA" with Iris's memoir.

Alex weaves his leftist ideas into the science fiction story. As the couple goes along inventing the plot, they repeatedly point out to each other that the included details have already happened, e.g. in ancient Mesopotamia. Alex bases his stories on written texts and mainly draws on the Bible, the Assyrian Code of Hammurabi[146], and other historical accounts, such as those of Herodotus[147]. For example, after his description of the society in Sakiel-Norn on the planet Zycron, depicting the aristocratic Snilfards and the subdued Ygnirods, i.e. the smallholders, serfs, and slaves, Alex says: "It's in the Code of Hammurabi, the laws of the Hitties and so forth" ("BA" 17). Right at the beginning Alex remarks: "Stick a shovel into the ground almost anywhere and some horrible thing or other will come to light. Good for the trade, we thrive on bones; without them there'd be no stories" ("BA" 11). Alex stresses that by 'digging up the bones' of the past and forming them into re-created 'facts' or stories, history can and must be kept alive, and that literature is necessarily dependent on a system of pre-established codes and on traditions of art forms and of culture in general; Iris has a similar opinion:

> Why should we assume that anything in the past is ours for the taking, simply because we've found it? We're all grave robbers, once we open the doors locked by others. But only locked. The rooms and their contents have been

---

[146] Hammurabi was a ruler of Babylon (1793-1750 BC), the world's first metropolis. His code of laws, which was carved in a stone monument to be reared in public view, is the earliest known example of a written law in society. It was found in 1901 and is exhibited in the *Louvre* in Paris (for further information see Postgate 275ff, for example).
[147] the father of modern historiography

left intact. If those leaving them had wanted oblivion, there was always fire.
(*BA* 494)

Both *BA* and "BA" emphasise that in dealing with the past one has to plunge in a network of intertextual relations.

The Planet Zycron is "located in another dimension of space" and surrounded by seven seas, five moons and three suns, and by western mountains with tombs, "where wolves howl and beautiful undead women lurk" ("BA" 10). In its city, Sakiel-Norn, a blind assassin saves a mute sacrificial virgin, whose tongue has already been cut out and who is about to be raped by an aristocrat who has paid for this 'privilege' to a High Priestess. After the rape the girl is to be sacrificed for an imaginary God. Even though the blind boy has been hired to kill the mute girl, they both fall in love and escape. Their story mirrors the relationship between the unnamed lovers and the circumstances surrounding their affair. The couple constructs this plot to explain their relationship to each other: they implicitly discuss the social gap between them, and more explicitly speculate on possible endings for their affair. Intratextual references to Iris's memoir clarify that Alex must be the unnamed man in "BA". He is an orphan and a Marxist like Alex and has a special way of lighting his match. Iris and Laura find a list of 26 words he has left in their attic (*BA* 219-10), words which he uses in his science fiction stories: e.g. carchineal ("BA" 350); *Iridis hortz* frog, nacrod, ulinth ("BA" 351); tristok ("BA" 400); and most importantly, he uses "xenor" and "zycron" to label the two planets.

Alex weaves an ironic critique of the hierarchical arrangements and power politics of the 1930s into the science fiction plot within "BA" and also into the dime novels he writes. He expresses his bitterness about the class differences mainly in the *"First Thrilling Episode in the Annals of the Zycronian Wars"* ("BA" 399), a story about intergalactic warfare between the Zycronians and the Lizard men of Xenor, which Iris spots in a drugstore after Alex has left for the war. The city of Sakiel-Norn is about to be invaded by the barbarians when spaceships with armed Xenorians land; in order to resist their advanced weaponry, the inhabitants of Sakiel-Norn and the barbarians decide to overcome class differences, the fear of the other and start to fight for common cause. Iris hurries home, locks herself in the bathroom and is eager to find out how Alex let their constructed science fiction story end; however, the blind assassin does not even appear in the story, and the plot is "rather Bolshevik": "Barbarians and urbanites, incumbents and rebels, masters and slaves – all forget their differences and make common cause. Class barriers dissolve [...]. All salute to each other by the name of *tristok*, which means (roughly), *he with whom I have exchanged blood*, that is to say comrade, or brother" ("BA" 400). While during their meetings Alex and Iris construct the fictitious story to explain their relationship to each other, Alex makes up a different science fiction plot to suit the expectations of the workers who read dime novels, and to get across his left-wing ideas.

The 1930s are a time Atwood is particularly interested in; she thinks "we're coming back to them" for "on a global scale today, there are a few rich countries with lots of power and desperately poor countries with none at all" (interview by Reynolds 21). The social inequalities of the 1930s culminated in the Second World War and the present-day effects of globalisation do not seem very promising, either. In an interview by Metzler Atwood stresses how important it is in contemporary societies to imagine what it is like to be another person: "The United States should try to imagine what it is like to be Saddam Hussein. Because if you can see the problem from the point of view of the other person, you have a much better chance of resolving it" (144). In her opinion, by studying meta/fiction, readers can become aware of how they themselves are fictionalising, i.e. what they make up of other people and what is 'real' (interview by Metzler 149). How the readership tends to fictionalise the context of an author's work will be explained in the following chapter.

7.1.2. *The Blind Assassin* by Laura Chase

Laura's novel depicts a sexual relationship between an unnamed wealthy woman, who the readers take to be Laura, and a man who is not her husband; thus, it becomes a scandal. After the publication of this book Iris has to continue her life in an even longer "shadow cast by Laura" (*BA* 41). Her husband Richard Griffen is forced to end his political ambitions and found dead in his sailboat. As Iris later reveals, she sent him a copy of Laura's novel, which is found next to his corpse; because of this Richard's sister Winifred (Freddie) accuses her of killing him. Iris suggests he committed suicide.

Iris points out that Laura's novel gets banned and how this resulted in an increase in book sales. The same has been happening to Atwood's *HT*[148]. Atwood comments that "nothing increases book sales more than to get yourself banned somewhere" and that "if it's a book with any power, there's always going to be some form of uproar" (interview by Reynolds 25). Iris explains that what the people remember about Laura's book

> isn't the book itself, so much as the furore: ministers in church denounced it as obscene, not only here; the public library was forced to remove it from the shelves, the one bookstore in town refused to stock it. There was word of censoring it. People snuck off to Stratford or London or Toronto even, and obtained their copies on the sly, as was the custom then with condoms. Back at home they drew the curtains and read, with disapproval, with relish, with avidity and glee – even the ones who'd never thought of opening a novel before. There's nothing like a shovelful of dirt to encourage literacy. (*BA* 39)

Fifty years after Laura's death, however, there is a growing academic interest in her work, mainly because her novel is being categorised under *Neglected Masterpieces of the Twentieth Century*" (*BA* 283). Due to a rewriting of literary canons Laura is now among "the most important female mid-century writers" (*BA* 287). Iris sarcastically remarks: "Laura was a 'modernist', we are told on the inside flap. She was influenced by the likes of Djuna Barnes, Elizabeth Smart, Carson McCullers[149] – authors I know for a fact that Laura never read" (*BA* 283). Throughout the novel Iris repeatedly compares Laura to "a tabula rasa, not waiting to write, but to be written down" and thus "it's only the book that makes her memorable now" (*BA* 46).

Iris notes that a work of literature is always re-created through the reading process and says that "what happens a set number of years after the death of the author" is that "you lose control. The thing is out there in the world, replicating itself in God knows how many forms, without any say-so from me" (*BA* 283). It is not the author who has authority over the meaning of a work of literature but it is the reader who re-creates the text through the reading process. This results in a continuous replication and various readings of one and the same text. Iris, however, does not like

---

[148] In Texas, for example, parents objected to their children reading the novel on school courses (interview by Reynolds 25).
[149] These were all women writers who had unconventional (sexual) relationships in their life. Their works are commonly interpreted through the lens of their biographies.

this idea, especially because after a life in the shadow of her sister Laura, she wants "only a listener perhaps; only someone who will see [her]" (*BA* 521).

She is fed up with the bombardment of scholarly requests she receives, asking for "manuscripts, mementoes, interviews, anecdotes – all the grisly details" (*BA* 286), and she has also given up replying to letters asking for help with proposed theses, overdue biographies, or any other sort of commemoration. Unlike Iris, Laura has achieved cult-hero status. Her sudden and tragic death has attributed to the novel's fame. Fans leave flowers on her grave or even scrap up "dirt from the grave" (*BA* 47). Iris remarks it is good that she did not bury the silver box containing Laura's ashes as "some fan would have pinched it by now. They'll nick anything, those people" (*BA* 47).

About the readers of Laura's novel, Iris says: "They wanted to finger the real people in it – apart form Laura, that is: her actuality was taken for granted. [...] Above all they wanted to know: *who was the man?* In bed with the young woman, the lovely, dead young woman; in bed with Laura" (*BA* 40). After reading "BA", Iris's own daughter, Aimee, believes that Laura and Alex are her real parents and that Iris therefore has no right to see Sabrina as she is not her grandmother (*BA* 436). Readers might be inclined to try to match a work of fiction with the author's life, which is evidenced in *BA* through a juxtaposition of Iris's memoir and Laura's novel. The people who knew Laura judged and characterised her anew considering that the novel was signed in her name, even though Laura certainly "had no thought of playing the doomed romantic heroine" and "became that only later, in the frame of her own outcome and thus in the minds of her admirers" (*BA* 417).

7.2. Self-Reflexive Narrators

Iris is a self-reflexive narrator, and an artist who impersonates all three identities of The Triple Goddess. As has been explained in chapter 5.2.2., the Triple Goddess is seen in three phases: "virginity, fecundity, and hag" (Patton 30); in her memoir Iris depicts her Diana and Hecate identity and the interspersed extracts of "BA" describe her Venus identity. Patton points out that even though Graves' White Goddess is "a figure descended from earth mothers and grain goddesses from the matriarchal past, she often eats children, sometimes even her own" (30). Old Iris plays with this image when she says to Myra: "should any of the wee ones disappear, I don't want to be accused of having lured them in and eaten them [...]. She thought I was making a joke" (*BA* 202). It is through writing her memoir that Iris attempts to transform her image as cold Hecate (or Crone) into one of a harmonious Triple Goddess.

The novel's self-reflexivity consists – among other features – in narratorial comments in the frame narratives of both *BA* and "BA". Iris reflects on the limits and possibilities of biographical reconstruction, while she is engaged in the writing process and the two unnamed narrators of Laura's novel are vividly discussing and commenting on their science fiction plots. At the beginning Iris does not have an exact audience in mind: "For whom am I writing this? [...] Perhaps I write for no one. Perhaps for the same person children are writing for, when they scrawl their names in the snow" (*BA* 43). Towards the end she emphasises that she writes her (fictional) autobiography for Sabrina, who is presently in India. Sabrina can be considered an intratextual version of the projected reader: she stands for the future generation of readers and for the reading public in general. This is stressed when Iris says in the last chapter: "What is it that I'll want from you? [...] only a listener perhaps; only someone who will see me. Don't prettify me though, whatever else you do: I have no wish to be a decorated skull" (*BA* 521).

Iris repeatedly reflects on the artifice and constructed nature of her writing, which at times results in a double-voiced discourse (graphically represented by the use of italics): "On this page, a fresh clean page, I will cause the war to end – I alone with a stroke of my black, plastic pen. All I have to do is write: *1918. November 11. Armistice Day*" (*BA* 75). At a later stage she points out: "It would be trite to say that this event changed everything, but it would also be true, and so I will write it down: *This event changed everything*" (*BA* 86). At times her narrative voice even merges with or foregrounds the product itself, for example when she says: "I feel like a letter – deposited here, collected there. But a letter addressed to no one" (*BA* 169), or when she points to projected versions of author and reader: "I must admit it's a surprise to find myself still here, still talking to you. I prefer to think of it as talking, although of course it isn't: I'm saying nothing, you're hearing nothing. The only thing between us is this black line: a thread thrown unto the empty page, into the empty air" (*BA* 473).

According to Viner, Atwood's *BA* "could almost be read as a plea not to confuse the author [Margaret Atwood] with the narrator [Iris Chase]". Rather than a plea it is a guide to reading works of fiction and in doing so, the world around us.

Readers of *BA* must work out for themselves how much of Laura's novel is really fiction and how much of it is part of reality, i.e. how much relates to its realistic frame (Iris's memoir). Analysing how these two layers relate to each other is also a guide to how we are fictionalising our lives, i.e. how we relate to external reality. Atwood is playing with the reader's assumptions right from the beginning, repeatedly reminds the reader of the framed narratives and stresses that some versions of all the ones that make up 'truth' are invisible for they lie under the surface (see "This Is a Photograph of Me").

Right at the beginning of the narrative Iris reflects on Laura's symbolic gesture of wearing white gloves when she drove the car off the bridge: "The white gloves: a Pontius Pilate gesture. She was washing her hands of me. Of all of us" (*BA* 2). While suggesting that Laura was washing her hands in 'innocence', i.e. that she was not guilty but driven by others to commit suicide; this biblical reference also anticipates a discussion of the notion of truth which meanders through the whole novel. Before Jesus was crucified, he was taken to Pontius Pilate, who "therefore said unto him, Art thou a king then? Jesus answered, Thou sayest that I am a king. To this end was I born, and for this cause came I into the world, that I should bear witness unto the truth. Every one that is of the truth heareth my voice" (John 18:37-8). And Pilate answered with the crucial question: "What is truth?" to emphasize that truth cannot be pinned down easily (John 18:38). In *Negotiating* Atwood discusses the differences between oral story-telling and writing; she points out that

> Jesus is a tale-teller. He teaches by parable, but he doesn't write a word, because he himself *is* the Word, The Spirit that bloweth where it listeth; he is fluid and intangible, like the speaking voice. But among his enemies are the Scribes and Pharisees – those that hold to the letter of the law – the written down letter[150]. Ironic, considering that we learn about all of this from a book. (47)

As our Past, the grand narrative, is only made of paper, "truth is sometimes unknowable, at least by us" (*In Search of* AG 37). This leads into a discussion of the problems of historical and biographical reconstruction.

---

[150] "[…] and what they wrote took on a fixed and unchanging quality" (*Negotiating* 47).

7.3. Reconstructing One's Past: An Overlapping of Art and Life

> Biography first convinces us of the fleeing of biography.[151]
>
> It's the very things that are not mentioned that inspire the most curiosity in us.[152]

Atwood defined any novel's essential characteristics as follows: "The novel as a form, is about time. [...] Time, money and love are the three central subjects of the novel, with time and money, being the constraints, and love being the thing that once in a while transcends them. But if you have time, you also have, eventually, death" (interview by Reynolds 24). Deery points out that Atwood enjoys to play with "the time-space of the form in which she is writing" (478):

> Her work reminds us that (written) literature has always spatialized time in that the book form spreads a narrative's beginning, middle, and end before its readers all at once: While the convention is to read the text sequentially, readers can dip in at any point. Atwood's narratives realize this potential for spatialization by interlacing past and present occurrences, so that even when reading sequentially the reader feels past and present events coexist (in space and time) together. (Deery 478)

Iris's memoir is recounted in flashbacks, from the fictional present to past events. The flashbacks are chronological but the continuous jumps between the outermost level of narration and the other layers remind the reader that the past is presented from her perspective in the present time. Iris recollects her memories from the collected papers and newspaper clippings in her steamer trunk, which symbolises her 'trussed' past made of paper: "That's my trousseau [...]. All at once it was a threatening word – so foreign, so final. It sounded like *trussed* – what was done to raw turkeys with skewers and pieces of string" (*BA* 238). For Iris self-discovery is possible by remembering these collected past experiences: from the point of view of an adult, she reconstructs her past in light of the present in order to come to terms with the influence of past events on her present self. But, as has already been mentioned in the analysis of *LO*[153], from a psychoanalytical point of view memory only "functions like a muse creating fictive pasts" and thus the process of self-discovery is "rather a process of

---

[151] Emily Dickinson in one of her letters (qtd. by Gudrun Grabher, Innsbruck University, in her lecture on "American Poetry")
[152] *In Search of* AG 19
[153] see chapter 6.2.

self-creation" and therefore an overlapping of art and life or an anti-mimetic attitude (Schier 3).

When Iris eventually decides to write down her life, so that her granddaughter Sabrina, who has been raised by Iris's sister-in-law Winifred, is given another perspective to the history of her family, she openly admits that her account is highly subjective – as any attempt at writing history will be. Implicitly scrutinising the notion of truth, she asks herself if what she remembers is "the same thing as what actually happened" and concludes: "it is now: I am the only survivor" (*BA* 218). No one can argue against her perspective and portrayal of events; however, even though Iris has complete authority over her story, this does not necessarily result in a 'true account':

> The only way you can write the truth is to assume that what you set down will never be read. Not by any other person, and not even by yourself at some later date. Otherwise you begin excusing yourself. You must see the writing as emerging like a long scroll of ink from the index finger of your right hand; you must see your left hand erasing it. Impossible, of course. (*BA* 283)

She also knows that her own picture of her family's history has been mediated through the perspective of their housekeeper Reenie. Iris recalls that the stories Reenie would tell her "varied in relation to [her] age, and also in relation to how distracted she was at the time" (*BA* 67). She goes on to say:

> In this way I collected enough fragments of the past to make a reconstruction of it, which must have borne as much relation to the real thing as a mosaic portrait would to the original. I didn't want realism anyway: I wanted things to be highly coloured, simple in outline, without ambiguity, which is what most people want when it comes to the stories of their parents. They want a postcard". (BA 67)

Iris is both "obsessed with memory and truth" and "wildly unreliable and secretive" (Showalter 142), which results in gaps in her selective account of her life to be filled by the reader. She makes clear that such gaps may carry meaning as well: "What isn't there has a presence like the absence of light" (*BA* 395). After she has recounted the relationship of her parents, for example, she pauses to reflect:

> How do I know all these things? I don't know them, not in the usual sense of knowing. But in households like ours there's often more in silences than in what is actually said – in the lips pressed together, the head turned away, the quick sideways glance. The shoulders drawn up as if carrying a heavy weight. (BA 79)

Iris constantly calls attention to the fabricated nature of her-story, especially because she reconstructs it from her memory, recollections from her steamer trunk. Through Iris's memoir Atwood points out that the attempt to look back at past events and turn them into 'facts' always results in a subjective narrative, as an understanding of past events depend on one's position in time and space. Deery stresses that "art doesn't capture the past, nor does time freeze art. The past is gone, and art keeps on changing" – also changing our understanding of the past, one should add (481).

In an interview by Hammond Atwood says: "You can only indulge in the luxury of figuring out yourself when you're oriented in space and time. Canada was a [colonised] country that lacked such an orientation" ("Articulating the Mute" 110). If we understand Iris as colonised in a patriarchal society, there is evidence that she lacks such an orientation because she has been relegated to the margin and 'silenced' by male discourse. In the same interview Atwood further claims that it is the desire of women to say "We exist [...]. We don't particularly wish to be defined by you" (110). In her memoir Iris eventually speaks up and tells her-story, which contradicts the public opinion about her. The picture readers get of Iris as a child, young woman, and old lady is constructed by gaps, by means of indirect characterisation, and through the novel apparently written by her sister Laura.

7.4. Marys and Marthas and the Duplicity of the Author

Laura and Iris are almost twins in physical appearance. Once Iris remarks: "Seeing [Laura] from behind gave me a peculiar sensation, as if I were watching myself" (*BA* 389). As regards their characters they are opposites who complement and depend on each other; in this sense, they symbolise the dualistic nature of human beings. After Iris's return from her honeymoon, they welcome each other holding on "tightly to each other's hands – left in right, right in left" (*BA* 313). Atwood holds the opinion that

> duality particularly interests fiction as a form. [...] Look at Christianity – having had God, they had to have the Devil. I think it's the structure of the body and the brain. Two hands, two eyes, two halves of the brain – but one heart. This has been something that has interested people, writing about being human. If we were millipedes, had a thousand legs and compound eyes, we'd write quite different books. (qtd. in Viner 8)

Iris and Laura are both loving sisters and fierce rivals for they love the same man, Alex Thomas. As Laura seems to symbolise the spiritual side and Iris the physical one, the sisters resemble – only on a surface level – biblical Mary and Martha in Luke 10:38-42: In this passage Jesus and his disciples are visiting the home of Mary and Martha in Bethany. While Martha is rushing about, concerned with the preparations for the meal, Mary is listening to Christ, ignoring her sister's angry side-way glances. When Martha complains to Jesus that her sister does not help her, he emphasises that women should put their spiritual responsibilities ahead of their physical ones and answers: "Mary has chosen what is better, and it will not be taken away from her" (Luke 10:41-2). Iris mocks this passage from the Bible when she describes the time when the sisters were hiding Alex in the attic at Avilion:

> We were Mary and Martha, ministering to – well, not Jesus, even Laura did not go that far, but it was obvious which of us she had cast in these roles. I was to be Martha, keeping busy with household chores in the background; she was to be Mary, laying pure devotion at Alex's feet. (Which does a man prefer? Bacon and eggs, or worship? Sometimes one, sometimes the other, depending how hungry he is). (*BA* 216)

It is one of the many instances in which Iris stresses that the spiritual and physical side cannot be separated and that even though the sisters have their misunderstandings they do need each other. They are opposites which form a whole: they belong together.

For his story of the Peach Women of the Planet Aa'A, Alex draws on the Mary and Martha story, too: "Both had hair the colour of a split-willow basket. [...] One of the girls was a sexpot, the other was more serious-minded and could discuss art, literature, and philosophy, not to mention theology" ("BA" 352-3). He mocks this passage by drawing on the incident when the sisters were hiding him in the attic and by projecting 'spiritual' Laura and 'man-eating' Iris into the story. Iris stresses: "You're wrong about the Peach Women though. They aren't the way you think" ("BA" 356). She rejects being cast into only one of these roles and stresses that they are inseparable in any woman.

She also stresses that the sisters are inseparable or even duplicitous when she argues that "BA" was the sisters' collaborative work. Towards the end of *BA* Iris explicitly states that 'Laura's novel' was not written by Laura and that Iris projected herself into the unnamed woman in "BA":

> Laura didn't write a word of it. But you must have known that for some time. I wrote it myself, during my long evenings alone, when I was waiting for Alex to come back, and then afterwards, once I knew he wouldn't. I didn't think of what I was doing as writing – just writing down. What I remembered, and also what I imagined, which is also the truth. I thought of myself as recording. A bodiless hand, scrawling across a wall. I wanted a memorial. That was how it began. For Alex, but also for myself. (*BA* 512)

Laura is not the author of "BA"; however, Iris stresses: "In another sense – what Laura would have called the spiritual sense – you could say she was my collaborator. The real author was neither one of us: a fist is more than the sum of its fingers[154]" (*BA* 512-3). Iris further states that for the reading public she herself, i.e. the 'real' author, is "only an appendage: Laura's odd, extra hand, attached to no body – the hand that passed her on, to the world, to them" (*BA* 287). Even though Laura might be the author or figure readers imagine standing behind the work, Iris stresses that the two of them are inseparable: "Laura was my left hand, and I was hers. We wrote the book together. It's a left-handed book. That's why one of us is always out of sight, whichever way you look at it" (*BA* 513).

When Iris stresses that "BA" was written by a duplicitous author, i.e. by both of the sisters, Atwood emphasises that any author is duplicitous for the hand which sets things down "is more than the sum of its fingers" as it is an intricate question who is in control of the hand at the moment of writing. The importance for perspective and abandoning conventional modes of perception in order to see is also evidenced in the inclusion of the photographs in *BA*.

7.5. Photographs: Mimetic or Distorting Mirror of Reality?

There are several photographs in BA, which raise the readers' awareness of conventional modes of perception. For example, when Iris looks at her own wedding picture, she observes a woman "casting too dark a shadow across her eyes" (*BA* 239):

> I say "her," because I don't recall having been present, not in any meaningful sense of the word. I and the girl in the picture have ceased to be the same person. I am her outcome, the result of the life she once lived headlong; whereas she, if she can be said to exist at all, is composed only of what I

---
[154] This proverb is also quoted in "BA" ("BA" 401).

> remember. I have the better view – I can see her clearly, most of the time. But even if she knew enough to look, she can't see me at all. (BA 239)

In an interview by Sharon Wilson Atwood expresses her interest in a photograph's ability to freeze time and to "freeze characters in roles that are socially conditioned, desired or feared" (qtd. in Deery 452). The wedding photograph is such an example which freezes time (and Iris's socially conditioned role as wife of prominent industrialist). From a retrospective point of view Iris can no longer identify with the person she once was, and young Iris cannot look into the future and foresee things. More important regarding the overall interest of the novel are, however, two prints of one and the same event, which underline the relationship between the sisters and give an additional explanation of the notion of authorship.

A week after Alex has left, Laura gives Iris a print of the photograph of the three of them at the picnic with herself cut out, only part of her hand – tinted in "a very pale yellow" – is still visible (*BA* 220). Iris remembers that then "the sight of Laura's light-yellow hand, creeping towards Alex across the grass like and incandescent crab, gave [her] a chill down the back of [her] spine" (*BA* 220). To Iris's question why she cut herself out, Laura gives a simple answer: "Because that's what you want to remember" (*BA* 220). Laura admits that she has another print of the same event with Iris cut out, i.e. another version of the truth she herself would like to keep in mind. At a much later stage Iris considers this "the closest she ever came, in my hearing, to a confession of love for Alex Thomas. Except for the day before her death, that is. Not that she used the word *love*, even then" (*BA* 220). Judging from her present-day perspective as an old woman, Iris knows she "ought to have thrown this mutilated picture away, but didn't" (*BA* 220). This incident splits the two sisters apart.

Each of the sister's keeps her own version of the past she would like to remember. The photographs show them on each side of the man they admire, Alex Thomas, a radical Marxist and – as revealed in "BA" – a writer of pulp-fiction. In each of the two copies the other sister's hand, scissored off at the wrist, is visible. On the one hand, these photographs are "mutilated" versions of reality and yet, they reveal that each of the sisters 'has a hand' in the other's relationship with Alex; furthermore, they emphasise that each of the sisters has been 'amputated' and lost their ability to feel or keep in touch with the other.

The prologue to "BA", *Perennials for the Rock Garden*, begins with a description of one of these mutilated photographs, namely Iris's. The unnamed woman in "BA", who we have identified as Iris, keeps it hidden in an envelope between the pages of a book about gardening, entitled *Perennials for the Rock Garden*[155]. The photograph depicts a man and a woman sitting under an apple tree – maybe under the (apple) Tree of Knowledge in the Garden of Eden. At first, Iris only says "it might have been an apple tree" ("BA" 4); in the epilogue, however, she is sure that "it must have been an apple tree" ("BA" 517). The epilogue depicts Laura's print and also reveals the central aspect of the photograph: one third has been cut off and the hand which is visible is "the hand of the other one, the one who is always in the picture whether seen or not. The hand that will set things down" ("BA" 517).

Iris stresses that the photographs depict happiness but that in life eternal happiness is not possible: "The picture is of happiness, the story is not. Happiness is a garden walled with glass: there's no way in or out. In Paradise there are no stories, because there are no journeys. It's loss and regret and misery and yearning that drive the story forward, along its twisted road" ("BA" 518). This resounds in "BA" when Alex tells the story about the Peach Women of Aa'A, who can read the space soldiers' minds and care for continuous harmony. The soldiers Will and Boyd, however are only happy until they realise that they cannot leave the place: "It's Paradise, but we can't get out of it. And anything we can't get out of is Hell" ("BA" 355). Alex keeps telling sad stories and when Iris complains, he answers: "Taken to its logical conclusion, every story is sad, because at the end everyone dies. Birth, copulation, and death" ("BA" 349). He stresses that it is the true-to-life stories which are worth being repeated: "All stories are about wolves. All worth repeating, that is. Anything else is sentimental drivel" ("BA" 344).

---

[155] This reference is further evidence that the narrative voice must be Iris's figural perspective. She has been given this book by Winifred and she takes it with her when she leaves Richard (see *BA* 501).

7.6. Foreshadowing and Epiphany

Several childhood experiences foreshadow what is ultimately happening to Laura, e.g. her plunge into the river on the day of their Mother's funeral and her accusation that Mr Erskine sexually molested her. Iris is continuously held responsible for Laura, especially because the family considers Laura incapable of looking after herself. According to Reenie, Laura is "the type to panic and thrash around and drown in six inches of water, through not keeping her head" (*BA* 143), which foreshadows her plunge into the river. When Laura falls in the Louveteau river, Iris shakes her and accuses her of having jumped in on purpose. Laura wails she did it "so God would let Mother be alive again" (*BA* 151). As Laura was told that Jesus died for our sins, she considered it to be possible to sacrifice her life for her mother's. After this incident Iris remarks:

> I couldn't get out of my mind the image of Laura, in the icy black water of the Louveteau – how her hair had spread out like smoke in a swirling wind, how her wet face had gleamed silvery, how she had glared at me when I'd grabbed her by the coat. How hard it had been to hold on to her. How close I had come to letting go. (*BA* 151)

Just like Laura tried to sacrifice her life for her mother then, she will later sacrifice herself again and endure "the pain and suffering" caused by Richard's sexual abuse in order to save Alex (*BA* 487).

Laura's behaviour towards Mr Erskine foreshadows how she will later behave towards Richard. When Richard says he will take her into his home, Iris remembers: "Laura didn't thank him. She stared at his forehead, with the cultivated blankness she had once used on Mr Erskine, and I saw we were in for trouble" (*BA* 316). She treats Richard in the same manner in which she behaved to Mr Erskine, a man who allegedly sexually molested her. One day Laura tells her sister that Mr Erskine "only wants to put his hand up [her] blouse […] or under her skirt. What he likes is panties" (*BA* 164). At that stage Iris cannot think of a sensible reason why a grown-up man should do any of that sort to a little girl like Laura. When Iris suggests telling Reenie, Laura answers: "She might not believe me. You don't" (*BA* 165). Reenie, however, does believe her and finds a way to get rid of Mr Erskine. After his departure, Laura decides to become a nun, upon which Iris remarks: "A little incredulity would have been a first line of defence" (*BA* 167). This foreshadows that her literal interpretation of the Bible and her blind belief in the substance of words is one of the reasons for her death (see chapter 7.8.2.). Several intertextual references foreshadow events, too; these will be treated in the following chapters. The intertextual analysis concentrates mainly on intertexts which serve to discuss the theme of (sacrificial) suicide and sexual politics.

7.7. On the Use of Intertextuality and Intertexts

7.7.1. Introductory Remarks

Many intertextual references discuss the theme of suicide and thus anticipate events, warning the reader of Laura's tragic death. *BA* is also replete with numerous allusions to other writers and books, for example in the detailed depiction of the books in Grandfather Benjamin's library, which establishes his Victorian cultural context, or in the depiction of the works on bookshelves in the rooms where Iris meets Alex, and in the naming of the literature that has made up the sisters' formal education. Wherever collections of literary works are depicted, they give an indirect characterisation of the character who owns or has read them, depict the character's attitude towards art, and establish or underline the character's cultural context.

Furthermore, the quoted novels are often examples of works that have contributed to establishing literary conventions in respective periods, or that were revolutionary in their time. The rooms in which the young 'unconventional' lovers meet in "BA" are often filled with avant-garde literature. In one place, for example, the book-shelf is filled with: "Auden, Veblen, Spengler, Steinbeck, Dos Passos. *Tropic of Cancer*, out in plain view, it must have been smuggled. *Salammbô*, *Strange Fugitive*, *Twilight of the Idols*, *A Farewell to Arms*. Barbusse, Montherlant. *Hammurabis Gesetz: Juristische Erläuterung*" ("BA" 123). Like Laura's novel, Henry Miller's *Tropic of Cancer*[156], was banned because of its explicit sexual adventures. Bradbury considers Miller "a crucial reminder that the novel of radical extremity took other than directly social form in the Thirties" and a forerunner of post-war experimentalism and postmodernism: "Miller's refusal to write a 'book' was a deliberate assault on all established concepts of art, and above all to the notion

---

[156] first published in Paris in 1934 and in New York in 1961

of literary responsibility and social allegiance" (147). Looking at the works, the figural medium Iris remarks: "She can tell by the books [...] that this friend would be hostile to her on principle" ("BA" 123). In *Tropic of Cancer* "the women are static, the hero dynamic" (*SW* 222); whereas the narrator in Miller's novel describes his sexual adventures from his point of view, "BA" is sexual explicit in giving a female point of view.

The formal education of Iris and Laura underlines their inept equipment for their future lives. Iris summarises the content of Mr Erskine's Latin lessons as consisting of

> selections from Virgil's *Aeneid* - [Mr Erskine] was fond of the suicide of Dido – or from Ovid's *Metamorphoses*, the parts where unpleasant things were done by the gods to various young women. The rape of Europa by a large white bull, of Leda by a swan, of Danae by a shower of gold – these would at least hold our attention, he said, with his ironic smile. (*BA* 163)

Maybe on purpose, Mr Erskine leaves out the rape of Philomela by Tereus for she and her sister have a cruel way of taking revenge (see chapter 7.7.9.).

With the teacher Miss Violence, Laura is left to colouring books and Iris studies literature of Romanticism and Victorianism and several of FitzGerald's quatrains, for example the following (*BA* 156-6):

> A Book of Verses underneath the Bough,
> A Jug of Wine, a Loaf of Bread - and Thou
>   Beside me singing in the Wilderness -
> Oh, Wilderness were Paradise enow![157]

The first version of FitzGerald's (1809-83) *The Rubáiyát of Omar Khayyám*[158] was published in 1859. Quotations from this work in *BA* are references to the fifth version, which was first published in 1889. Iris is puzzled that "Edward FitzGerald hadn't really written it, and yet he was said to be the author" (*BA* 156). In fact, he did not translate Khayyám's quatrains literally but "rendered" them into English, as he was careful to point out in the preface to the second edition of 1868. According to Haight, the quatrains are new creations by FitzGerald (8). Iris stresses that the name

---

[157] see also FitzGerald 125, Quatrain 12
[158] Omar Khayyám was a 12th century Persian poet and astronomer. *Rubáiyát* is "the plural of the Arabic word *rubá-íyáh*, a quatrain or stanza of four lines" (FitzGerald 171). In *Negotiating* Atwood quotes the poet Earle Bingley who claimed in the 1950s that "most Canadians had only three hardcover books in their house: the Bible, the works of Shakespeare, and Fitzgerald's *The Rubáiyát of Omar Khayýam*" (6).

on the title of a book is no guarantee that the person is also the author, and that the contents are not necessarily 'original' but draw on or use other texts. As FitzGerald's work shows, there can be a fine line between translation, source, and intertext.

FitzGerald's Quatrain 12, is repeated in the first chapter of "BA" when Alex mockingly transforms it to fit the present situation of Iris and him sitting on a park bench and having a picnic; he says: "A bottle of lemonade, a hard-boiled egg and Thou" and Iris finishes "beside me singing in the public park" ("BA" 11). The two of them continuously allude to and subvert literary texts to mirror their personal situation. At another instance Alex mocks a phrase from Wordsworth's "Daffodils" (1807), namely "[...] that inward eye/ Which is the bliss of solitude" to use it in his science fiction plot:

> Men ... are always called X. Names are no use to them, names only pin them down. Anyway, X is for X-ray – if you're X, you can pass through solid walls and see through women's clothing. But X is blind, she says. All the better. He sees through women's clothing with the inner eye that is the bliss of solitude. ("BA" 118)

The discussions of the young lovers expose literary conventions, inasmuch as they lay bare the construction of the science fiction plot. Both their story-telling to each other and Iris's comments in her memoir treat intertextuality as a theme.

7.7.2. Washroom Graffiti

Iris is fascinated by washroom graffiti, an example of intertextuality 'in practice' in contemporary society. Atwood thinks that "the writer of books, like the graffiti artist, is freer than the tale-teller: he doesn't stick around for feedback" (*Negotiating* 48). Readers as re-creators of texts are here free to interact with texts and add their own perspective to them. The washroom in the doughnut shop "offers inscriptions" which are not painted over frequently and "thus you have not only the text but the commentary on it as well" (*BA* 84). Iris's current favourite sequence is the following:

> *Don't Eat Anything You Aren't Prepared to Kill.* (engraved deeply in the paint)
> *Don't Kill Anything You Aren't Prepared to Eat.* (in green marker)
> *Don't Kill.* (in ballpoint)
> *Don't Eat.* (in purple marker)
> *Fuck Vegetarians - "All Gods Are Carnivorous" - Laura Chase.* (in bold black lettering). (*BA* 84)

As fans quote from her sister's novel, Iris concludes that "thus Laura lives on" (*BA* 84). This example of graffiti also underlines the fact that an artistic work is not a fixed product but a process in which readers may collaborate. Graffiti foregrounds the human urge for communication and being remembered. Iris elaborates on this when she says:

> Why is it we want so badly to memorialize ourselves? Even while we are still alive. We wish to assert our existence, like dogs peeing on fire hydrants. We put on display our framed photographs, our parchment diplomas, our silver-plated cups; we monogram our linen, we carve our names on trees, we scrawl them on washroom walls. It is all the same impulse. What do we hope from it? Applause, envy, respect? Or simply attention of any kind we can get? At the very least, we want a witness. We can't stand the idea of our voices falling silent finally, like a radio running down. (*BA* 95)

At times Iris feels "a strong urge to join in, to contribute; to link [her] own tremulous voice to the anonymous chorus of truncated serenades, scrawled love letters, lewd advertisements, hymns and curses" for "isn't it what they want? What we all want: to leave a message behind us that has an effect, if only a dire one; a message that cannot be cancelled out" (*BA* 420). She notes down one of FitzGerald's quatrains:

> The Moving Finger writes, and, having writ,
> Moves on; nor all your Piety nor Wit
>   Shall lure it back to cancel half a Line,
> Nor all your Tears blot out a Word of it.[159]

FitzGerald's Quatrain 71 is a direct reference to the Book of Daniel. Biblical myth has it that a disembodied hand appeared to scribble a prophetic and coded message of the fall of Babylon on the wall (Daniel 5:5-30). This quotation underlines the image of the duplicity of any author, symbolised by "The Double as Cut-Off Body Part" and stresses the power of the written word (*Negotiating* 43). Iris underlines this when she says that her writing hand takes on a life of its own: "Sometimes it seems to me that it's only my hand writing, not the rest of me; that my hand has taken on a life of its own, and will keep on going even if severed from the rest of me [...]" (*BA* 373).

---

[159] FitzGerald 146, Quatrain 71

7.7.3. History and/as Intertext

The past is made of paper.[160]

Linda Hutcheon distinguishes between *metafiction* and *historiographic metafiction*. She argues that history appears to have a "double" or "contradictory" status: on the one hand, "what history refers to is the actual, real world (and what fiction refers to is a fictive universe)" and on the other hand, "you can also find [...] another view of history, [...] history AS intertext" in the sense that "history becomes a text, a discursive construct upon which literature draws as easily as it does upon other artistic constructs" (1987:169-70). This would lead us to the conclusion that history "could never have reference to any empirical world but merely to another text" (Hutcheon 1987:170).

Hutcheon points out that even though there were 'real' historical events and figures, "these are accessible to us only through textualized, interpreted 'reports'" (1987:171). She has therefore coined the term *historiographic metafiction* to label "fiction that is at once metafictional and historical in its echoes of both the events and the texts, the contents and the forms, of the past"[161] (1987:169). Historiographic metafiction is consciously self-reflexive and concerned with the question of historical knowledge: it questions the absolute 'knowability' of the past by blurring the distinction between fact[162] and fiction. Atwood remarks: "When I was young I believed that 'non-fiction' meant 'true.' But you read a history written in, say, 1920 and a history of the same events written in 1995 and they're very different. There may not be one Truth – there may be several truths –saying that is not to say that reality doesn't exist" (interview by Snell 2).

Atwood applies well-researched intertextual references to historical characters and events, and merges the historical events with the personal events in the life of Iris. The novel deals with the most important happenings in Canada in the twentieth-century and relates these to the Chase and Griffen families: the two world wars have an impact on the Chase family and its industries, especially because Norval Chase is the only son to return from World War I. The Chase family is further affected by

---

[160] *In Search of* AG 31
[161] Hutcheon stresses that the term *postmodernist* should be reserved for historiographic metafiction (1987:169).
[162] (Historical) Facts are events to which we have given meaning. This is why "different historical perspectives" may "derive different facts from the same events" (Hutcheon 1993:57).

political events such as the Great Depression, the fear of communism, and union activities which result in the button factory fire, a fire for which Alex is held responsible. These interrelations establish a link between political and personal events.

In Laura's novel the young couple draws upon historical accounts and ancient myths for their construction of the science fiction story. When Iris offers a suggestion how the blind assassin could lead the barbarians into the city of Sakiel-Norn, she adds that the plot she is drawing on is "in Herodotus, or something like that is. The fall of Babylon, I think it was" ("BA" 342). Her idea on how the blind assassin and his girl could be spared and lead a happy live ever after makes Alex protest that she cannot have the "twosome betray their own people" ("BA" 343). Iris answers: "It's history, she says. It's in *The Conquest of Mexico* – what's his name, Cortez[163] – his Aztec mistress, that's what she did. It's in the Bible too. The harlot Rahab did the same thing, at the fall of Jericho[164]. She helped Joshua's men, and she and her family were spared" ("BA" 343).

This exemplifies how our understanding of the past is dependent on written historical accounts and also how they are interdependent on each other. The young lovers mainly draw upon accounts and myths from Ancient Mesopotamia, the Bible, and historical writings. Biblical myth has it that The Garden of Eden was to be found in the basin between Tigris and Euphrates, i.e. the land called Mesopotamia. According to the documentary by Gardner, the accounts in the Old Testament, and especially the Book of Moses, draw upon myths of the peoples living in Mesopotamia: the Chaldaeans, Sumerians, Babylonians, and the Assyrians. Uruk, capital of the Sumerian Empire, gave birth to the *Epic of Gilgamesh*[165]. This Epic contains the mythical Flood, the Tree of Knowledge (as a tree of pomegranates), the snake which brings about the downfall, and various other elements. The discussions of the lovers are implicitly meta-intertextual for they take intertextuality as a theme to be explored and in so doing, they raise the readers' awareness of the interrelation of literary texts and cultural traditions.

---

[163] Iris refers to William Hickling Prescott's *History of the Conquest of Mexico, with a Preliminary View of Ancient Mexican Civilization, and the Life of the Conqueror, Hernando Cortes* (1843).
[164] see Joshua 6:1-27
[165] written about 2000 BC

Their discussions also underline that historiography is a subjective interpretation of historical events. Iris expresses this, too, when she says: "I don't know why anyone found it strange that [the natives] decorated the skulls of their ancestors, I thought. We do that, too" (*BA* 389). As interpreters of the 'bones' of the past, i.e. the historical events, we 'decorate' them by turning them into facts or rather faction[166]. In *RB* the character Antonia (Tony) Fremont, a professional historian, reflects on historical writing and "is daunted by the impossibility of accurate reconstruction" (461):

> Why bother [...] with such a quixotic notion as the truth? Every sober-sided history is at least half sleight-of-hand: the right hand waving its poor snippets of fact, out in the open for all to verify, while the left hand busies itself with its own devious agendas, deep in its hidden pockets. (461)

Before moving on to an analysis of individual intertexts, I would like to conclude this chapter with and important issue raised by Atwood in her published lecture *In Search of AG*:

> What does the past tell us? In and of itself, it tells us nothing. We have to be listening first, before it will say a word; and even so, listening means telling, and then re-telling. It's we ourselves who must do such telling, about the past, if anything is to be said about it; and our audience is one another. After we in our turn have become the past, others will tell stories about us, and about our times. (37)

Atwood stresses that as readers and thus re-creators of texts, we inevitably write history.

7.7.4. Fairy Tale Motifs

7.7.4.1. Sleeping Beauties in Their Rapunzel Tower

Laura and Iris spend their childhood in Avilion, "a merchant's palace" (*BA* 58). Avilion was christened by Iris's grandmother Adelia, who took the name from Tennyson's mythic *Idylls of the King*:

> The island-valley of Avilion;
> Where falls not hail, or rain, or any snow,

---

[166] a blending of fact and fiction

> Nor ever wind blows loudly; but it lies
> Deep-meadow'd, happy, fair with orchard lawns
> And bowery hollows crown'd with summer sea, ... (*BA* 61)

Iris suspects that people in town must have laughed at her for this quotation for "Avilion was where King Arthur went to die. Surely Adelia's choice of name signifies how hopelessly in exile she considered herself to be: she might be able to call into being by sheer force of will some shoddy facsimile of a happy isle, but it would never be the real thing" (*BA* 61). Just like Avilion has been a Rapunzel tower for Grandmother Adelia, it is one for Iris and Laura, too.

Iris and Laura are princesses in a secluded Victorian-style home, cut off from Canadian society: "There were only the two of us [...] on our thorn-encircled island, waiting for rescue; and on the mainland, everyone else" (*BA* 43). They are Rapunzel figures imprisoned in their tower of societal restrictions: marriage is the only profession open to them. This turns them into passive Sleeping Beauties waiting for their prince to rescue them. Both believe that Alex Thomas could be "the handsome prince" who comes to their aid. However, he rescues neither of the two sisters. In "BA" Iris asks herself: "How can she ever get out of it, her life, except through him?" ("BA" 409). Laura is sure that once the war is over and Alex returns, they will live happily ever after. When she is faced with her shattered illusions, she drives off a bridge. Iris wakes up when she faces her shattered illusions, symbolised by her dream of the destruction of Sakiel-Norn in "BA" (467-8); she knows she must acknowledge the fact that Alex is dead and take responsibility for her own life; Laura, however, cannot cope with his death and commits suicide.

7.7.4.2. *The Bluebeard Theme*

Zipes points out that "Bluebeard shows us a woman leaving the safety of home and entering the risky domain of her husband's castle" (56). Iris and Laura leave their safe and secluded home Avilion and enter Richard's castle. Richard is a patriarchal Bluebeard figure for he "keeps the keys to power and knowledge" while his two 'wives', Iris and Laura, are denied any choice in the matter of their own destiny (Reynolds & Noakes 8). Iris remembers that when he offered her the engagement ring, "he produced a small black velvet-covered box [...]. Inside was a glittering *shard* of light" (*BA* 228, *my emphasis*). Her marriage to Richard results in her subordination and emotional amputation, symbolised by the "shard of light". She has no money except through him; therefore, when Iris finds out that she is pregnant, she considers it advisable to stay with Richard and pretend it is his child even though Alex, who is about to leave for the Spanish Civil War and might not return, is the real father.

Bluebeard-Richard exerts all his power on Laura: he abuses her sexually and silences her by making her believe that Callie, a friend of Alex's, keeps him informed about Alex's hiding places; he threatens to immediately hand him over to the police should Laura not succumb to his will. When he finds out about her pregnancy he shuts her off in a mental institution and arranges the abortion; thus Laura is not only emotionally but also physically mutilated by Richard. Like the third sister in the Bluebeard tale, Iris puts the only remains of her sister, i.e. the "charred smithereens" (*BA* 1), back together by writing *BA*; the public images of Laura and Iris do not coincide with their real personalities. Iris recreates their stories to make them memorable for the future generation.

7.7.4.3. Girls without Hands

Atwood draws on the Grimm's tale "The Girl without Hands" to express how women are restricted or 'amputated' in a patriarchal society[167] and to underline the theme of incest or sexual abuse, which is one of the reasons for Laura's death. The Grimms' tale goes back to a version in which a father wants to marry his daughter after the death of his wife. When she refuses, he cuts off her hands (and breasts) and chases her off into the world (McGlathery 101). In the Grimms' tale the father promises his daughter to the devil[168], who in the course of the story forces the father to chop off his daughter's hands. Renate Meyer zur Capellen cites this fairy tale as an example of "how folk tales reflect men's feelings about women, and the position of women, in a male-dominated society" (qtd. in McGlathery 111).

Wilson points out that the protagonists in Atwood's fiction are often symbolically denied hands (1996:55), which symbolises their emotional amputation. Judging from their "mutilated" hands on the photographs, Iris and Laura seem to be

---

[167] See Atwood's poem "The Girl without Hands" from the poetry collection *Morning in the Burned House* (1995).
[168] Incest equals offering her to the devil (McGlathery 111).

missing their sense of touch. The photograph taken at the Labour Day Picnic shows that one of each sister's hands has been amputated. After their encounter with Alex, both Iris and Laura seclude themselves in their worlds of imagination and do not share their thoughts with the other sister anymore for "there was too much that could not be said, on either side" (*BA* 221).

In a sense, it is Norval Chase who sells his daughters off to the 'devil' Richard when the latter promises the infusion of capital on the condition that he is given Chase's daughter Iris (and after their father's death also Laura) and the remains of the estate. For both sisters this marriage results in emotional isolation: Laura is emotionally amputated because sexually abused by Richard, and Iris remarks: "Laura touches people. I do not" (*BA* 192). From early childhood on neglected in favour of Laura, Iris has learned to seclude herself in a world of emotional isolation: "She's the round O, the zero at the bone. A space that defines itself by not being there at all" ("*BA*" 409).

When Iris leaves Richard, she deposits a letter for him, in which she claims to have evidence that he abused Laura and threatens "if he had any ideas about getting his filthy hands at Aimee [...] he should discard them, because [she] would then create a very, very large scandal [...]" (*BA* 502). Even though she attempts to prevent her daughter from the influence of Richard and Winifred, the odds – and eventually also Aimee – are against her. After Aimee's death, she says: "I mourned the self she'd been at a much earlier age. I mourned what she could have become; I mourned her lost possibilities. More than anything, I mourned my own failures" (*BA* 437). Iris mourns her passive existence and that she has not taken active responsibility for herself, Laura, and Aimee.

7.7.5. Samuel Taylor Coleridge's "Kubla Khan"

As a child Iris goes through the bookshelves in her Grandfather's library, which contain literature expressing Grandmother Adelia's idea of what Grandfather Benjamin "ought to have read" (*BA* 155). Iris picks out a couple of books that interest her and juxtaposes the first two lines from "Kubla Khan" to the beginning from the war poem "In Flanders Fields"[169] by John McCrae (1872-1918): *"In Xanadu did Kubla Khan, A stately pleasure-dome decree. In Flanders fields the poppies blow, Between the crosses, row on row"* (*BA* 155). Atwood contrasts these lines to express the social gap in society: while some people are living in "pleasure domes," others live in poverty and have suffered from the war.

The Canadian poet John McCrae, a medical officer in WW I, wrote the poem to describe the horrors of the second battle in the Western Front (the Ypres salient) in the spring of 1914. His poem commemorates the deaths of thousands of soldiers who died in Flanders during the war[170]. Grandfather Benjamin, even though "not a war profiteer in that sense" (*BA* 70), did profit from the war: "War is good for the button trade. So many buttons are lost in a war, and have to be replaced – whole boxfuls, whole truckloads of buttons at a time. They're blown to pieces, they sink into the ground, they go up in flames" (*BA* 71). The lines also differentiate the world in which Iris and Laura are living from the life of Alex Thomas, who dies in World War II, and most importantly, the lines juxtapose poetic imagination and harsh reality.

Coleridge's poem is subtitled "A Vision in a Dream: A Fragment." His claim in the Preface to "Kubla Khan" that the poem came to him in an opium dream is famous but also questionable (Barnard 96). It might be due to its fragmentary nature that "reaching any consensus about the poem's meaning has been problematical" (Leask 1); however, critics commonly emphasise that it elaborates on the nature of poetic inspiration and imagination (Barnard 96-7). The poem opens with the emperor Kubla Khan, who decrees the building of a pleasure dome. This dome is located in an enchanted, exotic place (a far-away romantic setting), where a woman cries for her demon-lover and the sacred river Alph – maybe the river of poetic inspiration – meanders five miles before plunging through caverns into a lifeless ocean. In the second part of the poem (ll. 37-54) a newly introduced "I" (the poetic genius) has a vision of an Abyssinian maid playing on her dulcimer[171]; he would imaginatively recreate in his imagination the Khan's dome if he could recapture his vision of "her symphony and song" (l. 43). The artist (poet) who could accomplish this would be regarded with awe and even fear by those from whom he is separated by his inspiration.

---

[169] first published in *Punch* (6 Dec. 1915) and later in his poetry collection *In Flanders Fields and Other Poems* (1919)
[170] Emory University, <http://www.emory.edu/ENGLISH/LostPoets.html, April 19, 1997>.
[171] music as the source for poetic inspiration

Fulford identifies the Khan as "a male figure of power [...] a conqueror, a statesman, a master-builder," and the poetic genius mentioned in l. 38 as someone who "builds domes in air, or the imagination" (1-2). Both figures are associated with a woman: "the Khan with 'the woman wailing for her demon lover' [l. 16] and the poet with the Abyssinian maid, who sings rather than wails" (2). He further stresses that critics cannot agree whether "Kubla Khan is analogous to, or contrasts with, the sublime poet" (3). The figures are associated and yet apart for Coleridge's poem consists of two interrelated layers, i.e. an outer 'realistic' frame in which the Khan has a dome built, whereas the poet's imaginative re-creation of the dome only consists in the fiction of an inner layer: the poet could recreate Kubla Khan's 'real' dome only "in air" (l. 46) if he could recapture the vision of his muse, the Abyssinian maid.

Under the motto of "Xanadu" Winifred organises a charity costume ball. Iris remarks that "people at that time liked costumes [...] almost as much as they liked uniforms. Both served the same end: to avoid being who you were, you could pretend to be someone else" (*BA* 332). Laura seems rather interested in the meaning of the poem and asks Iris to give her a sensible interpretation but her sister has to admit: "I didn't know the answers to any of these questions. I know all of them now. Not the answers of Samuel Taylor Coleridge – I'm not sure he had any answers, since he was hopped up on drugs at the time – but my own answers. Here they are, for what they're worth" (*BA* 334):

> The sacred river is alive. It flows to the lifeless ocean, because that's where all things that are alive end up. The lover is a demon-lover because he isn't there. The sunny pleasure-dome has caves of ice because that's what pleasure-domes have – after a while they become very cold, and after that they melt, and then where are you? All wet. Mount Abora was the Abyssinian maid's home, and she was singing about it because she couldn't get back to it. The ancestral voices were prophesying war because ancestral voices never shut up, and they hate to be wrong, and war is a sure thing, sooner or later. Correct me if I'm wrong. (*BA* 334)

Iris gives her very personal and subjective interpretation of the poem: she sees the river as the River of Life which flows into the ocean (a symbol of death); the lover Alex is a demon-lover because he died (and both Iris and Laura are wailing for him); in her past she has lived in sunny pleasure-domes: in Avilion, which has been sold and made into an old-age home called Valhalla[172] and which she sees as "Ambition's mausoleum [...] now" even though "it was once thought imposing in its way – a merchant's palace" (*BA* 58); then she lived in Richard's palace, a place inside which she learned to construct her own 'pleasure-dome': "The pleasure-dome was where I really lived now – where I had my true being, unknown to those around me. With walls and towers girdled round, so nobody else could get in" (*BA* 335). All pleasure-domes, however, have fallen apart: first Avilion, then Iris has to face her shattered illusions. She built up her own 'pleasure-dome' when she cut herself off from the outside world and had illusions of escaping with Alex, illusions which she knows were not realistic and destined to melt[173] (see "BA" 463-5). Like Joan Foster in *LO*, Iris attempts to escape from harsh reality and retreat into the secluded world of imagination. For both Joan and Iris this isolation from reality results in emotional isolation only.

Like the Abyssinian maid, Iris cannot get back to her home Avilion for it belongs to her husband after her father's death; Iris suffers from haunting dreams about ancestral voices: "When you're young you think everything you do is disposable. [...] You think you can get rid of things, and people too – leave them behind. You don't yet know about the habit they have, of coming back. Time in dreams is frozen. You can never get away from where you've been" (*BA* 396). While she is haunted by guilt, there might be another reason for why she hears ancestral voices: in *Negotiating* Atwood argues that all writing "is motivated deep down, by a desire to make the risky trip to the Underworld, and to bring something or someone back from the dead" (156):

> All writers learn from the dead [...] All writers must go from now to once upon a time; all must go from here to there; all must descend to where the stories are kept; all must take care not to be captured and held immobile by the past. And all must commit acts of larceny, or else of reclamation, depending how you look at it. The dead may guard the treasure, but it's useless treasure unless it can be brought back into the land of the living and allowed to enter time once more – which means to enter the realm of the audience the realm of the readers, the realm of change. (*Negotiating* 178-9)

---

[172] Iris remarks that "Avilion" turned into "Valhalla," an old-age home unsuitably named: "As I recall, Valhalla was where you went after you were dead, not immediately before" (*BA* 57).
[173] For the costume ball Iris dresses as the Abyssinian maid but without an essential garment, i.e. the dulcimer as the medium for her art, which underlines the fact that her illusions are shattered.

In this sense, "ancestral voices never shut up": the construction of art is an ongoing process if literature is recreated by readers.

Within the context of *BA* Coleridge's poem takes on a very specific meaning – at least for Iris who invites readers to "correct" her if she is wrong and add their own interpretations. The intertextual reference underlines Iris's emotional isolation: she has built up her fictitious pleasure-dome inside Richard's Rapunzel tower of societal restrictions.

7.7.6. Giacomo Puccini's *Turandot*[174]

The night before the wedding of Iris and Richard, Laura comes into Iris's bathroom, barefoot and in a white night-gown, which makes her look "like a penitent – like a heretic in an old painting, on her way to execution" (*BA* 136). She sprays herself with Iris's perfume and begs her sister not to marry Richard. Iris justifies her decision by saying that they need to be taken care of financially since the factories are closed and "Avilion is falling to pieces" and adds that she has got her eyes open (*BA* 237). Laura answers that they are only open like those of a "sleepwalker" and pointedly expresses Iris's state of mind: while the elder sister believes to be conscious of the events, Laura already understands that she has been blinded by the prospect of "nice clothes" and that she lives in her dream world and is thus ignorant of the events going on around her (*BA* 237).

In her wedding night Iris uses the same perfume, which is called *Liù*, "a scent [she] found frail and wan. It was named […] after a girl in an opera – a slave girl whose fate was to kill herself rather than betray the man she loved, who in his turn loved someone else" (*BA* 241). Iris considers such a plot typical of the fictitious world of operas, but sleepwalking through real life, she is ignorant of the plot concocted by Richard, whose schemes result in Laura's "fatal, triangular bargain," i.e. her bargain with God to endure Richard's sexual abuse in order to save Alex. When they meet for the last time, Laura explains to Iris: "I had to make the sacrifice. I had to take the pain and suffering onto myself. That's what I promised God. I knew if I did that, it would save Alex" (*BA* 487). Iris comments that Laura had "the infuriating iron-clad confidence of the true believer" (*BA* 487). She supposes that

---

[174] It was first performed at the *Teatro della Scala* in 1926.

Alex must have been the father of Laura's child, who Richard had arranged to be aborted in the mental institution; feeling jealous, she makes clear to Laura that her bargain did not save Alex for he died in World War II and she cannot help adding that they had an affair. By telling her this, Iris (like Turandot) intensifies Laura's torture.

Liù is a character from Puccini's opera *Turandot*, which is based on a dramatised fable by the same name written by Carlo Gozzi[175]. The plot revolves around Princess Turandot's promise to marry whoever can answer three riddles that she poses. Her suitor Calaf, a handsome prince, succeeds, the princess begs her father not to abandon her to a stranger, and Calaf generously offers Turandot a riddle of his own: if she can learn his name by dawn, he will forfeit his life. Liù, a slave girl, endures torture and rather kills herself than reveal the name of her secret love, Calaf (who, unfortunately, is captivated by Princess Turnadot's beauty instead). Turnadot is impressed by the girl's endurance during the torture and asks her what it is that gives her the strength to endure physical pain rather than reveal the name of Turandot's suitor, upon which Liù replies that it is "love" (Act III). When the Princess signals to intensify the torture, Liù snatches a dagger from one of the soldiers and kills herself[176]. She sacrifices her life for the prince she loves. Eventually, Turandot becomes aware of her own physical passions and concedes to marry her suitor Calaf; however, even though Turandot and Calaf mourn for Liù, they were, after all, the reason why Liù killed herself.

While in Puccini's opera Liù is sacrificed for the better good, i.e. for unification between Calaf and Turnadot, Atwood fills the gaps in the opera by focusing on the perspective of the sacrificial slave girl. Laura, who appears like the scent of the perfume "frail and wan" (*BA* 241), can be identified with Liù for she endures Richard's abuse and kills herself rather than betray her prince Alex, who has an affair with Iris, the "Snow Queen" Turandot[177]. The central enigma in *BA* is why Laura commits suicide and whether she does it of her own account or is pushed by

---

[175] Gozzi's play was first performed in 1761 and is in turn adapted from *The Arabian Nights* (Zipes 408).

[176] Puccini's opera ends with Liù's death for he died of cancer before he could finish the last act; the ending as usually performed nowadays was completed by Franco Alfano, using Puccini's notes and sketches (*Harenberg* 665).

[177] See the aria sung by Liù in Act III: *"Tu, che di gel sei cinta"*; Iris, too, secludes herself emotionally from those around her and especially from her sister.

others. Turandot and Calaf do not prevent Liù from killing herself, and Iris (and probably also Alex) are blind to Laura's suffering.

7.7.7. Alfred Lord Tennyson's "Mariana in the Moated Grange" and "Break, break, break"

With Miss Violence, their private tutor, Iris and Laura study the Victorian poet Alfred Lord Tennyson (1809-83), "a man whose majesty was second only to God's, in the opinion of Miss Violence" (*BA* 155-6):

> With blackest moss the flower-plots
> Were thickly crusted, one and all:
> The rusted nails fell from the knots
> That held the pear to the gable-wall ...
> She only said, "My life is dreary,
> He cometh not," she said;
> she said, "I am aweary, aweary,
> I would that I were dead!"

The first verse from "Mariana in the Moated Grange"[178] draws upon Shakespeare's *Measure for Measure*. Mariana waits in a grange for her lover, who has deserted her; when she knows he will not come back, she commits suicide. In the second stanza Mariana "could not look on the sweet heaven" just as Dido "is weary of gazing on the arch of heaven" in Virgil's *Aeneid*, IV 451 (qtd. in Abrams 1057). The poem – the first stanza and the refrain especially – foreshadow the circumstances for Laura's suicide. She waits for Alex's return from the war and when Iris tells her that he died and will not come back, she, too, commits suicide. Not yet initiated into the adult world, Laura does not understand why the woman in the poem wishes to be dead. Miss Violence, a spinster lost in romantic illusions (and significantly an advocator of art for art's sake), explains that it was because of "boundless" but "unrequited love" and adds that "a poem does not reason why" (*BA* 156).

As an adolescent woman Iris later recalls: "The poems that used to entrance me in the days of Miss Violence now struck me as overdone and sickly. *Alas, burthen, thine, cometh, aweary* – the archaic language of unrequited love" (*BA* 389). She

---

[178] first published in *Poems, Chiefly Lyrical* (1842). The hints for character and situation are found in Shakespeare's *Measure for Measure* III i, 277 (see *Norton*, Vol. 2, 1057-8).

resists the image of "Victorian sacrificial maidens [...] whose only solution to unrequited love was a passionate love-death" (Staels 78). Her memoir is to reconstruct the image of her sister, who has become a death cult, too.

Iris reads another of Tennyson's poems during Miss Violence's lessons, i.e. "Break, break, break"[179] (*BA* 156), which he wrote in memory of his friend Arthur Hallam, who had died abroad in 1833[180]:

1   Break, break, break,
On thy cold gray stones, O Sea!
2   And I would that my tongue could utter
The thoughts that arise in me.

Iris is standing at the railing of the *Berengeria*, crossing the ocean over to Europe on her honeymoon with Richard. Watching the ocean, she is reminded of this poem but cannot recall the exact words: "I tried to remember something I might have read about [the ocean], some poem or other, but could not. *Break, break, break.* Something began that way. It had cold grey stones in it. *Oh Sea*" (*BA* 246).

An analysis of Tennyson's words gives an inside view into Iris's mind. Tennyson's poem expresses grief over the death of a beloved person. The speaker, standing at the sea-shore describes the power of the ocean, a literary symbol for death. He watches the waves breaking on the stones, an image which evokes his breaking heart, i.e. his heart crumbling to pieces and being washed away by the waves. The exclamation "O" might be more than a sigh of sorrow: the letter designates a hole, i.e. a minus-quantity, standing both for death (the ocean) and for silence, i.e. that which cannot be represented in words.

Both the speaker of this poem and Iris, who recalls it, cannot translate their feelings into words: just as he cannot express "the thoughts that arise" in him, Iris cannot express the pain she is going through, mainly because she seems not to be aware of her own emotions and only feels inner emptiness. On the night before her marriage she says: "I seemed to myself erased, featureless, like an oval of used soap, or the moon on the wane" (*BA* 235). The last three stanzas not quoted in *BA* are also revealing:

---

[179] first published in *Poems, Chiefly Lyrical* (1842)
[180] For the rest of his life Tennyson wrote poems expressing his grief, including his famous elegy *In Memoriam A.H.H.* (1850).

4	O, well for the fisherman's boy,
	That he shouts with his sister at play!
6	O, well for the sailor lad,
	That he sings in his boat on the bay!
8	And the stately ships go on
	To their haven under the hill;
10	But O for the touch of a vanish'd hand,
	And the sound of a voice that is still!
12	Break, break, break
	At the foot of thy crags, O Sea!
14	But the tender grace of a day that is dead
	Will never come back to me.

The description of the children playing (ll. 4-5), the sailor singing and mending his boat (ll. 6-7), and of the stately ships portrays the daily lives of people oblivious to the speaker's grief. While the speaker's heart is quietly breaking, others are going about their normal lives. Iris longs for the touch of Laura's "vanish'd hand". In another sense, through marrying Richard, Iris's hands have been amputated, and she longs to recapture her inner self, her emotions, which she feels have been "erased" (*BA* 235). Iris knows, too, that "the tender grace of a day that is dead/ Will never come back to [her]".

These lines express her momentary feelings but they also anticipate how she will feel as a lonely old woman. After she finds her sister's message Iris says: "How can I describe the pool of grief into which I was now falling? I can't describe it and so I won't try" (*BA* 500); however, like Tennyson, she will feel the need to write about the loss of a beloved person: first, when she writes "BA" to conserve in memory Alex and the dimension where she was most happy, and then when she writes *BA* to make herself memorable and transform herself from "the round O, the zero at the bone", a "space that defines itself by not being there at all" into a substance visible to others in the form of her memoir ("BA" 409).

7.7.8. Virgil's *Aeneid*: Dido's Suicide (Book IV)

After Laura has taken Iris's car keys of Iris to drive the car over the bridge, she leaves a message for her sister in the attic; this message consists of five books, "the books of knowledge" (*BA* 498). In Laura's Latin notebook, Iris finds a translation of the concluding lines of Book IV of Virgil's *Aeneid*, a translation Laura had made with the help of Iris. Dido, Queen and founder of Carthage, falls in love with Aeneas, who is cast ashore with his crew. In Book IV she starts a liaison with Aeneas. The Gods fear that a relation with Dido might distract Aeneas from his destiny in Italy and so Mercury is sent to order Aeneas's departure. Dido begs him to stay but he chooses war instead of her love. After he has sailed away, Dido is mad with grief, builds a pyre inside the palace, and commits suicide. Iris remarks that "although bleeding like a stuck pig, Dido is having a hard time dying" (*BA* 498). Laura's translation of the concluding lines of Book IV of Virgil's *Aeneid* goes like this:

> Then powerful Juno felt sorry for her long-time sufferings and uneasy journey, and sent Iris from Olympus to cut the agonizing soul from the body that still held onto it. This had to be done because Dido was not dying a natural death or one caused by other people, but in despair, driven to it by a crazy impulse. Anyway Proserpine hadn't yet cut off the golden lock from her head or sent her down to the Underworld./ So now, all misty, her wings yellow as a crocus, trailing a thousand rainbow colours that sparkled in the sunlight, Iris flew down, and hovering over Dido, she said:/ As I was told to do, I take this thing which belongs to the God of Death; and I release you from your body./ Then all warmth stopped at once, and her life vanished into the air. (*BA* 498-9).

Just like the Goddess Iris ends Dido's pain and suffering, it seems that Iris ends Laura's pain and suffering, when she pushes her sister off by telling her that Alex Thomas died in the war, and that the two of them had an affair. She is taken by surprise when her sister takes her car keys; her car is the means for Laura to commit suicide. Like Dido, Laura sees suicide as the only solution to end her misery.

The theme of suicide, or sacrificial maidens, permeates the whole novel. As an old lady Iris recounts how she watched a young woman set fire to herself:

> What possesses them, these young girls with a talent for self-immolation? Is it what they do to show that girls too have courage, that they can do more than weep and moan, that they too can face death with panache? And where

does the urge come from? Does it begin with defiance, and if so, of what? Of the great leaden suffocating order of things, the great spike-wheeled chariot, the blind tyrants, the blind gods? Are these girls reckless enough or arrogant enough to think that they can stop such things in their tracks by offering themselves up on some theoretical altar, or is it a kind of testifying? (*BA* 433)

Iris considers such an act only "admirable [...] if you admire obsession" and "completely useless" (*BA* 433). She draws parallels to Laura's suicide when she says that she certainly does not hope that this woman wanted "to atone for the sins of her money-ridden, wrecked, deplorable, family" (*BA* 433).

While writing her memoir, Iris points out that her garden adjoins the Louveteau Gorge, in which "once in a while there's a corpse, whether fallen or pushed or jumped is hard to tell, unless of course there's a note" (*BA* 50). There is no note when her daughter Aimee is found at the bottom of the stairs with her neck broken and Iris says: "Fallen or pushed or jumped, we'll never know" (*BA* 434). Iris also points out how the relatives tend to suffer from "sideway looks" when a young woman commits suicide and remarks that she's "sure they're blameless, but they're alive, and whoever's left alive gets blamed" (*BA* 473). She experiences this herself when Reenie and Aimee accuse her of being responsible for Laura's death.

At a later stage she remembers Reenie's ideas about people committing suicide. When the body of the woman who jumped off the Jubilee Bridge above the rapids was found, it "was far from a pretty sight because going down those rapids was like being run through a meat grinder. Not the best way to depart this earth, said Reenie – not if you were interested in your looks, though most likely you wouldn't be at such a time" (*BA* 141). Reenie's ideas about suicides reveal her stereotypical way of thinking:

> As well as jumping, said Reenie, women like that might walk into the river upstream and then be sucked under the surface by the weight of their wet clothing, so they couldn't swim to safety even if they'd wanted to. A man would be more deliberate. They would hang themselves from the crossbeams of their barns, or blow their heads off with their shotguns; or if intending to drown, they would attach rocks, or other heavy objects – axe-heads, bags of nails. They didn't like to take any chances on a serious thing like that. But it was a woman's way just to walk in and resign herself, and let the water take her. (*BA* 141)

Iris attempts to reconstruct the public image of her sister Laura because "whether fallen or pushed or jumped is hard to tell, unless of course there's a note" (*BA* 50). Rumour has it that Laura committed suicide, which turns her into a (death) cult figure. Iris wants to prevent Laura from becoming a woman who simply resigned and let herself be washed away by the water. Her memoir novel is this note, the written record, which clarifies whether Laura fell, was pushed, or jumped: the explanation *BA* offers is that it was a combination of falling, pushing, and jumping. Like the Greek Goddess[181] in the *Aeneid*, Iris had a hand in Laura's death; as messenger of the gods it is her duty to tell the true story about her sister.

7.7.9. Carpet Weaving as Story Weaving: "Philomela's Artefact"
Everyone walks into the maze blindfolded.[182]

The word *text* derives from Lat. *textere, textum*, meaning 'to weave', 'woven' (Cuddon 963); in this sense, a text is like a 'woven fabric,' just like Atwood's novel is a woven fabric of various genres, which gives a composite picture of reality. This underlines the constructed nature of language and art and points to the fact that language or art mediates our knowledge of reality. The plot of *BA* (and also of "BA") recalls Tereus's rape and mutilation of his sister-in-law Philomela in Book VI of Ovid's *Metamorphoses* (6,451ff).

Ovid recounts the myth as such: Tereus, King of Thrace is married to Procne, the daughter of Pandion, King of Athens. Tereus is immediately attracted by his sister-in-law Philomela. On their way to Thrace he rapes the virgin and then cuts out her tongue so that she cannot tell anyone about the crime. He leaves her in a strongly guarded place and tells his wife Procne that her sister died on the journey; however, Philomela manages to convey what happened to her by weaving the events into a tapestry which she has sent to her sister. One year later, Procne 'reads' her sister's cloth, frees her, and together they take revenge on Tereus[183]. Philomela finds a way to

---

[181] Iris, the winged Goddess of the Rainbow and God's messenger, was the goddess who separated the soul from the body after death; since the soul exits through the eyes, the coloured part was named after her (Fink 155).
[182] *Negotiating* xviii
[183] They kill his son and serve him to Tereus.

communicate with her sister as she makes herself heard through art; she has recorded past experiences in her artefact.

Like Philomela, Laura is sexually abused and silenced. Richard silences her by ensuring her belief that sacrificing herself to him is the only way how she can save Alex, and once more later when he has her confined to a mental asylum as he fears his public position could be threatened should she reveal her pregnancy. Like Procne, Iris is blind to her sister's torture and made to believe in a lie. Richard and Winifred tell her that Laura is insanely jealous of Iris and only imagines being pregnant. Iris suspects that the father, "whether imagined or real", can only be Alex Thomas (*BA* 441). She also admits that she did not know her sister any longer: "She had become unknown to me, as unknown as the inside of your own glove is unknown to you when your hand is inside it. She was with me all the time, but I couldn't look at her. I could only feel the shape of her presence: a hollow shape, filled with my own imaginings" (*BA* 441).

When Laura reveals her pregnancy to a doctor at the hospital where she is engaged in charity work, the doctor informs Richard who has her confined to the mental institution. Laura must have already suspected that she is in danger of being shut out of harm's way and thus taken precautions. She has left a message for Iris and has Reenie tell her sister she'd know where to find it (*BA* 445). However, when Iris finds Laura's message, which is – like Philomela's – "not in words" (*BA* 450), she does not understand it. Laura has altered two of the wedding photographs: she has coloured herself in yellow, i.e. the colour of the sun, a life giving source. Iris cannot figure out what it means "this radiance [...] as if Laura was glowing from within" (*BA* 451); most likely, it symbolises her pregnancy, i.e. a life "glowing from within". She has obliterated Richard's features and painted his hands and face in flame-red, a colour symbolising sensuality, sexual desire and also blood; this hints at her sexual abuse and abortion. She has coloured Iris blue on one print, to express that she is lost in her imaginative world, i.e. sleeping and blind to events around her[184], and on the second print her face has been "fogged over", which symbolises her blurred perception of reality (*BA* 451).

It is only when Iris finds her sister's final message, "the books of knowledge", that she realises her ignorance of 'the message' that was before her eyes all along (*BA*

---

[184] When Iris catches her sister colouring the family portraits in the library, she ask Laura why she painted her face blue, upon which Laura replies: "Because you're asleep" (*BA* 195).

498-500). Laura had been trying to tell her sister what was going on but Iris was blind to her message. Like Procne, Iris is captivated by a feeling of hatred towards her husband and eager to take revenge. One thing Iris had learned from Mr Erskine was that "revenge is a dish best eaten cold. [She]'d learned not to get caught" (*BA* 167). She takes revenge by having "BA" published and signing it in Laura's name, which destroys Richard's political career, but this only results in her own isolation and the continuation of a life in Laura's shadow.

7.8. Concluding Remarks

7.8.1. "... only the blind are free": Freedom, Betrayal, and Guilt

> I have not done it justice, or rather mercy. Instead I went for vengeance. An eye for an eye leads only to more blindness.[185]
> As a rule, we tend to remember the awful things done to us, and to forget the awful things that we did.[186]

BA is replete with betrayals: Richard betrays Norval Chase when he closes down the factories and does not take care of his daughters after his death, Richard betrays Iris with Laura (and later with other women), he betrays both sisters by abusing and lying to them; Iris uses Richard to get away from Avilion and be relieved from the burden of Laura, Iris betrays Richard with Alex and by having an affair with Alex she also betrays Laura. Most importantly she betrays her sister by breaking her promise to look after her and by allowing herself to remain blind to her sister's suffering; Iris and Laura betray each other by not talking openly and secluding themselves in their imaginative worlds, and even the Gods cannot be relied on for Eros and Justitia betray all of them: "Eros with his bow and arrows is not the only blind god. Justitia is the other one. Clumsy blind gods with edged weapons: Justitia totes a sword, which, coupled with her blindfold, is a pretty good recipe for cutting yourself" (*BA* 497).

The saying among the child slave carpet weavers in the science fiction story that "only the blind are free" ("BA" 22) alludes to Iris's blindness[187] for she is

---

[185] *CE* 443
[186] *In Search of* AG 8
[187] Karen F. Stein draws an intertextual relation between Atwood's novel and Emily Dickinson's "blonde assassin" in Dickinson's poem 1624.

Laura's "blind assassin": Iris is shut out of Laura's life by Richard and Winifred and made to believe that her sister is taken care of. Her love for Alex Thomas and her aspirations to lead a wealthy life also make her blind to Laura's needs. As an old woman she recalls seeing Alex in the streets of Toronto and asks herself if she could have changed the course of events:

> I could have paid no attention. I could have turned away. That would have been wise. But such wisdom was not available to me then. I stepped down off the curb and began to cross towards him [...]. In that moment I had already committed treachery in my heart. Was this a betrayal, or was it an act of courage? Perhaps both. Neither one involves forethought: such things take place in an instant, in an eyeblink. This can only be because they have been rehearsed by us already, over and over, in silence and in darkness; in such silence, such darkness, that we are ignorant of them ourselves. Blind but sure-footed, we step forward as if into a remembered dance. (*BA* 321)

Likewise, when Iris reflects on her reasons why she helped Laura to hide Alex in the attic, she considers: "Was it my belief that I was doing this only to spare her – to help her, to take care of her, as I had always done? Yes. That is what I did believe" (*BA* 211). Judging from her present-day perspective she knows that she did it for her own good.

Winifred is convinced that "BA" killed Richard and thus accuses Iris and Laura of killing Richard whereupon Iris asks: "Who killed Laura, then?" (*BA* 370), suggesting that he is responsible for Laura's death. For the rest of her life Iris is tortured by the feeling that she did not care for her sister. She is haunted by nightmares and when she tells the doctor that she dreams too much, he replies: "Must be a bad conscience" (*BA* 372). That Iris does feel responsible for her sister's death, becomes clear when she describes her feelings after Laura's plunge into the river, feelings she recounts after Laura tells her about her triangular bargain:

> I wanted to shake her. I closed my eyes for a moment. I saw the pool at Avilion, the stone nymph dipping her toes; I saw the too-hot sun glinting on the rubbery green leaves, that day after Mother's funeral [...]. Laura was sitting on the ledge beside me, humming to herself complacently, secure in the conviction that everything was all right really and the angels were on her side, because she'd made some secret, dotty pact with God. My fingers itched with spite. I knew what had happened next. I'd pushed her off. (*BA* 488-9)

She has literally pushed her sister off then and – in a metaphorical sense – she pushes Laura off the bridge in the end. Towards the end of "BA" and *BA* Iris asks herself how she could have been "so ignorant [...] so stupid, so unseeing, so given over to carelessness" even though everything "had been there all along, right before [her] very eyes" ("BA" 517; *BA* 500):

> But without such ignorance, such carelessness, how could we live? If you knew what was going to happen next – if you knew in advance the consequences of your own actions – you'd be doomed. You'd be as ruined as God. You'd be a stone. You'd never eat or drink or laugh or get out of bed in the morning. You'd never love anyone, ever again. You'd never dare to. ("BA" 517-8)

This is why only the blind are free. Iris offers this excuse for her actions and writes *BA* "to take care of [her]self [...] and Laura, as [she] solemnly promised to do. Better late than never" (*BA* 368).

7.8.2. "In the beginning was the word...": Laura's "fatal, triangular bargain"

> Touch comes before sight, before speech. It is the first language and the last, and it always tells the truth. This is how the girl who couldn't speak and the man who couldn't see fell in love.[188]

Iris explains that "as most small children do, Laura believed words meant what they said, but she carried it to extremes" (*BA* 86). On the day of their mother's funeral Laura is confident that "Mother is with God" (*BA* 96); Laura believed in the Holy Word "not in the double way everyone else believed them, but with a tranquil single-mindedness that made [Iris] want to shake her" (*BA* 96). In a sense, Laura's blind belief in the substance of words, in the descriptive fucntion of language, leads to her tragic end:

> In the beginning was the word, we once believed. Did God know what a flimsy thing the word might be? How tenuous, how casually erased? Perhaps this is what happened to Laura – pushed her quite literally over the edge. The words she had relied on, building her house of cards on them, believing them solid, had flipped over and shown her their hollow centres, and then skittered away from her like so much waste paper. (*BA* 490)

---

[188] "BA" 256

Iris enumerates what Laura relied on: "*God. Trust. Sacrifice. Justice. Faith. Hope. Love.* Not to mention *sister*" (*BA* 491). Laura counts on these words when she builds her illusions of a happy ending with Alex, illusions which do not coincide with reality. Thus, in a metaphorical sense, Iris does not lie to *The Toronto Star*, which writes: "Mrs Richard E. Griffen, wife of the prominent manufacturer, gave evidence that Miss Chase suffered from severe headaches affecting her vision" (*BA* 3). Laura blindly believes in the substance of words, in their reference to external reality; she trusts her illusions to become real for "God doesn't cheat" (*BA* 487). In a sense, this leads to her tragic end and is therefore a "fatal triangular bargain"[189] (*BA* 487).

---

[189] cf. Charles S. Peirce's triad of the linguistic sign

8. CONCLUSION

It has been shown that metafictional and intertextual features aim at a re/education of the reader, inasmuch as they play with the reader's horizon of expectations to subvert pre-established literary norms and deconstruct persistent ideologies. Metafiction and intertextuality raise the reader's awareness that there is no simple dichotomy between fact and fiction or reality and art. Atwood uses metafiction and intertextuality to warn the reader not to treat her novels as classic realist texts and interpret them according to codes appropriate for traditional realist literature, or, as Howells remarks, "her novels challenge her readers to see more by seeing differently" (3). Most importantly, Atwood's writings emphasise the importance of the reader as a re-creator of texts.

Atwood's self-reflexive narrators reflect on the relation between art and reality, the writing process, and on the end product, i.e. their works and the reception of these; in doing so, they lay bare their fictional status. In her novels Atwood combines prose and poetry, dreams, fairy tale motifs, myth, parody, and pastiche to deconstruct the certainties of traditional realism. Her multi-layered narratives exemplify how our perception of external reality is framed, for an outer layer always provides the 'realistic' framework for an inner layer. The study of meta/fiction can thus be a guide to how we are fictionalising our lives and external reality. In *LO* and *BA* the characters' crises result from their inability to disentangle fiction from reality: they are unable to see what is really there and what they have made up. Both self-reflexive narrators take responsibility in the end by telling or writing their stories.

LO and *BA* are two self-reflexive narratives in which metafiction and intertextuality are used to question the concept of mimesis and with it the possibility of describing and representing truth. By means of a self-reflexive narrator, multi-layered and interrelated narratives which all merge in the end, and through intertextual references the writings call attention to their fictionality. In *LO* Joan's Costume Gothics merge with her own life and in *BA* the merging of fiction and reality is expressed by the merging of socio-political events and personal events in the Chase family and more precisely, by the merging of the events in Iris's memoir with those in "BA" which in turn merge with the innermost science fiction plot. Once the various layers collide, both protagonists become aware of the extent to which they have been fictionalising their lives and how they have been blind to perceiving external reality.

The narratives comment on or even parody literary and popular art conventions to show how these conventions determine our notions of reality. Whereas *LO* discusses the relation between art and reality by depicting the role of a woman artist in Canada in the 1970s, the treatment of the same issue in *BA* is more complex and global: the latter novel discusses the relationship between fact and fiction in regard to knowledge of the past and 'truth' as 'absolute knowability'. In the novels analysed Atwood provides an/other perspective to the intertexts, points to the impossibility to fix meaning, stresses that "every myth is a version of the truth" (*LO* 106), or that truth is composite (*BA*). In *LO* the intertextual references are employed to discuss issues of story-telling and the role of a woman artist and her relationship to society. In *BA* the intertextual references stress that our past is made of paper, deconstruct the image of Victorian sacrificial maidens, or give an inside view into characters' minds. Atwood uses well-known pre-texts to guarantee communicativity and explicitly marks the intertextual references, sometimes even hinting at or providing an interpretation of the pre-text within her narratives.

Both narratives emphasise that history becomes an individual's her-story as past experiences shift and change depending on one's perspective or position in time and space. *BA* forces the reader to recognise the extent to which fiction or historiography determines human life and our understanding of the past. Historical events and historiography do play an intrinsic role in both novels, inasmuch as they are subsumed under a more specific treatment of an individual artist's her-story. In *LO* Joan is unaware of important historical events because so much secluded in her escapist fantasy world; her notion of history and of her own life is determined by the Costume Gothics she produces. *BA* questions theories of realism and historiography, and in particular the objectivity of the Press, as it shows the influence of present and past cultural and political contexts on writing history. The novel can be seen as rewriting history and, most importantly, a woman's her-story.

As has been shown, Atwood parodies conventions of the Gothic romance in *LO*. By using these conventions in Joan's memoir, and by mixing the discourse of popular romance with the poetic discourse of the "LO" poems, she tries to close the gap between the popular art of mass-culture and the high art of modernism to discuss not only literary conventions and traditions but also contemporary society. The extracts from the Costume Gothics and the prose poems "LO" reveal the extent to which Joan's perception of reality is determined by fiction. These embedded genres function to blur the boundary between reality and art in order to point to the constructedness of reality. Joan interprets her life and herself in terms of the conventions and stereotypes of popular literature, Hollywood films, fairy tales and myths about femininity. The self-reflexive and fragmentary *mise-en abyme* structure of the narrative symbolises Joan Foster's search for a unified self and the 'true' story. Eventually, she comes to terms with a multiple and many-faceted personality, as is suggested by her identification with the Triple Goddess and her determination to continue writing.

BA is more explicit in stressing how language determines our notions of reality, i.e. how it shapes our existence and experience. Alex and Iris explain their relationship to each other through the construction of a science fiction story, and Iris writes her scrap-book-like memoir by using the collected papers and clippings hidden in her steamer trunk, i.e. the remnants of her past made of paper. All layers in *BA* depict our dependency on written accounts for historical knowledge; they stress that truth is composite and also consists in what is left out. Unlike *LO*, *BA* also takes intertextuality as a theme to be explored as both Iris's memoir and the discussions of the couple in "BA" reveal an auto-reflexive consciousness of intertextuality.

After 23 years Atwood's employment of metafiction and intertextuality has become much more complex. The reason for this might have to do with a feature Atwood points out in *SW*:

> When you begin to write, you deal with your immediate surroundings; as you grow, your immediate surroundings become larger. There's no contradiction. When you begin to write, you're in love with the language, with the act of creation, with yourself partly; but as you go on, the writing – if you follow it – will take you places you never intended to go and show you things you would never otherwise have seen. I began as a profoundly apolitical writer, but then I began to do what all novelists and some poets do: I began to describe the world around me. (15)

Atwood deconstructs traditional conventions which aim at a mimetic representation of reality to produce narratives which raise the readers' awareness of how we fictionalise our lives and external reality. In doing so, she describes the world around us: "A piece of art, as well as being a creation to be enjoyed, can also be […] a mirror. The reader looks at the mirror and sees not the writer but himself; and behind his own image in the foreground, a reflection of the world he lives in" (*Survival* 15).

9. BIBLIOGRAPHY

9.1. Texts

9.1.1. Texts by Margaret Atwood

The Blind Assassin. 2000. London: Bloomsbury, 2000.
The Robber Bride. 1993. London: Virago, 2001.
Cat's Eye. 1988. New York: Bantam, 1996.
Lady Oracle. 1976. Toronto: Seal, 1999.

9.1.2. Other Texts

Andersen, Hans Christian. *Ausgewählte Märchen*. Wien: Carl Ueberreuter, 1947.
The Bible: Authorised King James Version. Ed. Robert Carroll. Oxford: OUP, 1997.
Coleridge, Samuel Taylor. "Kubla Khan: A Vision in a Dream." 1816. Rpt. In Abrams 346-9.
---. "The Rime of the Ancient Mariner." 1798. Rpt. in Abrams 330-46.
FitzGerald, Edward. *The Rubáiyát of Omar Khayyám*. Roslyn: Black, 1942.
Grimm, Jacob, and Wilhelm Grimm. *The Complete Grimms' Fairy Tales*. Trans. Margaret Hunt and James Stern. New York: Panteon, 1972.
Hardy, Thomas. *Tess of the D'Urbervilles*. 1891. London: Penguin, 1998.
Khalil, Gibran. *Der Prophet*. Trans. Giovanni und Ditte Bandini. München: dtv, 2002.
Miller, Henry. *Tropic of Cancer*. New York: Grove, 1961.
Ovid . *Metamorphosen*. Stuttgart: Reclam, 2001.
Puccini, Giacomo. *Turandot*. Orch. Philharmonique de Strasbourg. Perf. Montserrat Caballé, Mirella Freni, and José Carreras. Cond. Alain Lombard. EMI, 1994.
Tennyson, Alfred Lord. "The Lady of Shalott." *Poems, Chiefly Lyrical*. 1832 and 1842 [revised]. Rpt. in Martin 305-10.
---. "Mariana in the Moated Grange." 1830. Rpt. in Abrams 1057-8.
Vergil . *Aeneid*. Trans. Cecil Day-Lewis. London: Random House, 1952.

9.2. Criticism

9.2.1. Interviews with Margaret Atwood

"Interview with Margaret Atwood." Hay on Wye, Wales. 26 May 2001. By Margaret Reynolds. Reynolds & Noakes 11-25.

"Interview with Margaret Atwood." Aug. 1997. By Marylin Snell. <http://www.motherjones.com/mother_jones/JA97/visions.html, 2002>.

"Defying Distinctions." Interview with Margaret Atwood. By Karla Hammond. 1978. Rpt. in *Margaret Atwood: Conversations*. Ed. Earl G. Ingersoll. London: Virago, 1992. 99-108.

"Interview with Margaret Atwood." *Strong Voices: Conversations with Fifty Canadian Authors*. By Alan Twigg. Boston: Harbour, 1990. 6-11.

"An Interview with Margaret Atwood." By Jan Garden Castro. VanSpanckeren & Castro 215-32.

"An Interview with Margaret Atwood." By Karla Hammond. *American Poetry Review* 8:5 (1979): 27-9.

"Creativity: An Interview with Margaret Atwood." By Gabriele Metzler. *Zeitschrift für Kanada-Studien* 27.1 (1995): 143-50.

"Articulating the Mute." Interview with Margaret Atwood. By Karla Hammond. 1978. Rpt. in *Margaret Atwood: Conversations*. Ed. Earl G. Ingersoll. London: Virago, 1992. 109-20.

"*Publishers Weekly* Interviews Margaret Atwood on the Publication of *Lady Oracle*." By Beverly Slopen. *Publishers Weekly* Aug. 23 1976. Rpt. in Margaret Atwood. *Lady Oracle*. Toronto: Seal, 1999. 424-9.

9.2.2. Criticism by Margaret Atwood

Curious Pursuits: Occasional Writing 1970 – 2005. London: Virago, 2005.

Writing with Intent: Essays, Reviews, Personal Prose 1983 – 2005. New York: Carroll & Graf, 2005.

Negotiating with the Dead: A Writer on Writing. Cambridge: Cambridge UP, 2002.

In Search of Alias Grace*: On Writing Canadian Historical Fiction*. Ottawa: U of Ottawa P, 1997.

Strange Things: The Malevolent North in Canadian Literature. Oxford: Clarendon, 1995.

"Writing Philosophy." *Waterstone's Poetry Lecture.* Hay On Wye, Wales. June 1995. Rpt. <http://www.library.utoronto.ca/canpoetry/atwood/write.htm>.

"If You Can't Say Something Nice, Don't Say Anything At All." *Language in Her Eye: View on Writing and Gender by Canadian Women Writing in English.* Eds. L. Scheier, S. Sheard, and E. Wachtel. Toronto: Coach House, 1990. 15-25.

"Great Unexpectations: An Autobiographical Foreword." VanSpanckeren & Castro xiii-xvi.

Second Words: Selected Critical Prose. 1982. Boston: Beacon, 1984.

Survival: A Thematic Guide to Canadian Literature. Toronto: Anansi, 1972.

"The Rocky Road to Paper Heaven." <http://www.web.net/owtoad/road.html>.

"Spotty-Handed Villainesses." <http://www.web.net/owtoad/vlness.html>.

"Ophelia Has a Lot to Answer for." Lecture at the Stratford Festival. Sept. 1997. Rpt. <http://www.web.net/owtoad/ophelia.html>.

9.2.3. Other Criticism

Abrams, Meyer H., gen. ed. *The Norton Anthology of English Literature.* Vol. 2. New York, London: Norton, 1993.

Albinia, Alice. "Booker's Book: Better to Puzzle than to Understand." *The Hindustan Times Online* <http://www.hindustantimes.com/nonfram/101100/detOPIO3.asp>.

Allen, Graham. *Intertextuality.* London: Routledge, 2000.

Audi, Robert, gen. ed. *The Cambridge Dictionary of Philosophy.* Cambridge: Cambridge UP, 1999.

Baer, Elizabeth R. "Pilgrimage Inward: Quest and Fairy Tale Motifs in *Surfacing.*" VanSpanckeren & Castro 24-34.

Baldick, Chris. *The Concise Oxford Dictionary of Literary Terms.* Oxford: Oxford UP, 1991.

Barnard, Robert. *A Short History of English Literature.* Oxford: Blackwell, 1994.

Barthes, Roland. "The Death of the Author". Lodge 167-72.

Barzilai, Shuli. "Say that I Had a Lovely Face: The Grimm's 'Rapunzel', Tennyson's 'Lady of Shalott,' and Atwood's *Lady Oracle.*" *TSWL* 19.2 (2000): 231-54.

Benson, Stephen. "Stories of Love and Death: Reading and Writing the Fairy Tale Romance." Sceats & Cunningham 103-13.

Berger, John. *Ways of Seeing*. London: Harmondsworth, 1972.

Bradbury, Malcolm. *The Modern American Novel*. Oxford: Oxford UP, 1992.

Broich, Ulrich, and Manfred Pfister, eds. *Intertextualität: Formen, Funktionen, anglistische Fallstudien*. Tübingen: Niemeyer, 1985.

Broich, Ulrich. "Formen der Markierung von Intertextualität." Broich & Pfister 31 47.

Bromberg, Pamela S. "The Two Faces of the Mirror in *The Edible Woman* and *Lady Oracle*." VanSpanckeren & Castro 12-23.

Bronfen, Elisabeth. *Over Her Dead Body*. Manchester: Manchester UP, 1992.

Brookner, Anita. "Artfully Administered Shocks." *The Spectator* 7 Oct. 2000: 50.

Bühler Roth, Verena. *Wilderness and the Natural Environment: Margaret Atwood's Recycling of a Canadian Theme*. Tübingen: Francke, 1998.

Cannon, Damian. *"The Red Shoes*: A Review."
<http://www.film.u_net.com/Movies/Reviews/Red_Shoes.html>.

Clark, Alex. "Vanishing Act." *Guardian Unlimited* 30 Sept. 2000
<http://books.guardian.co.uk/reviews/generalfiction/0,6121,375154,00.html>.

Cooke, Nathalie. *Margaret Atwood: A Biography*. Toronto: ECW, 1998.

Cuddon, John A. *Dictionary of Literary Terms and Literary Theory*. London: Penguin, 1992.

Cude, Wilfred. "Nobody Dunnit: The Loose End as Structural Element in *Lady Oracle*." *Journal of Canadian Studies* 15.1 (1980): 30-43.

Currie, Mark. *Metafiction*. London: Longman, 1995.

Davey, Frank. "*Lady Oracle*'s Secret: Atwood's Comic Novels." *Studies in Canadian Literature* 5 (1980): 209-21.

Davidson, Arnold E., and Cathy N. Davidson, eds. *The Art of Margaret Atwood: Essays in Criticism*. Toronto: Anansi, 1981.

Deery, June. "Science for Feminists: Margaret Atwood's Body of Knowledge." *TCL* 43.4 (1997): 470-86.

Di Cesare, Mario. *The Altar and the City: A Reading of Vergil's* Aeneid. New York: Columbia UP, 1974.

Dvorak, Marta. "What Is Real/ Reel? Margaret Atwood's 'Rearrangement of Shapes on a Flat Surface' or Narration as Collage." *Etudes Anglaises* 51.4 (1998): 448-59.

Farron, Steven. *Vergil's* Aeneid: *A Poem of Grief and Love*. Leiden: Brill, 1993.

Fee, Margery. *The Fat Lady Dances: Margaret Atwood's* Lady Oracle. Toronto: ECW, 1993.

Findley, Timothy. "Margaret Atwood." *Encyclopaedia of Post-Colonial Literatures in English*. Vol. 1. Ed. Eugene Benson and L. W. Conolly. London: Routledge, 1994.

Fink, Gerhard. *Who's Who in der antiken Mythologie*. München: dtv, 2002.

Fogel, Stanley. "'And All the Little Typtopies': Notes on Language Theory in the Contemporary Experimental Novel." *MFS* 20 (1974): 328-36.

Fulford, Tim. "Mary Robinson and the Abyssinian Maid: Coleridge's Muses and Feminist Critcism." *Romanticism on the Net* 13 (1999) <http://users.ox.ac.uk/~scat0385/kublarobinson.html>.

Freibert, Lucy M. "The Artist as Picaro: The Revelation of Margaret Atwood's *Lady Oracle*." *Canadian Literature* 92 (1982): 23-33.

Gardner, Robert, dir. "Brennpunkt Bibel – Spurensuche in Mesopotamien." *Discovery* ZDF Feb. 17, 2003.

Godard, Barbara. "Structuralism/ Post-Structuralism: Language, Reality and Canadian Literature." Moss 25-51.

Grace (1984), Sherrill. "Courting Bluebeard with Bartók, Atwood, and Fowles: Modern Treatment of the Bluebeard Theme." *JML* 11.2 (1984): 245-62.

--- (1983). *Margaret Atwood: Language, Text, and System*. Vancouver: U of British Columbia P.

--- (1981). "Margaret Atwood and the Poetics of Duplicity." Davidson & Davidson 55-68.

--- (1980). *Violent Duality: A Study of Margaret Atwood*. Montreal: Véhicule.

Grant, Michael, and John Hazel. *Who's Who in Classical Mythology*. London: Weidenfeld & Nicolson, 1999.

Graves, Robert. *The White Goddess: A Historical Grammar of Poetic Myth*. London: Faber & Faber, 1952.

Haight, Gordon S. "Edward FitzGerald and the Rubáiyát." FitzGerald 3-18.

Harenberg Opernführer. Dortmund: Harenberg, 2000.

Helbig, Jörg. *Intertextualität und Markierung: Untersuchungen zur Systematik und Funktion der Signalisierung von Intertextualität.* Heidelberg: Winter, 1996.

Hill Rigney, Barbara. *Margaret Atwood.* London: Macmillan, 1995.

Houppert, Karen. "*The Blind Assassin* by Margaret Atwood," *Salon.com Books,* <http://www.salon.com/books/review/2000/09/12/atwood/>.

Howells, Coral Ann. *Margaret Atwood.* London: Macmillan, 1996.

Hutcheon (1993), Linda. *The Politics of Postmodernism.* London: Routledge.

--- (1988). *A Poetics of Postmodernism: History, Theory, Fiction.* New York: Routledge.

--- (1987). "History and/as Intertext." Moss 169-84.

Jensen, Emily. "Margaret Atwood's *Lady Oracle*: A Modern Parable." *Essays on Canadian Writing* 33 (1986): 29-49.

Jump, Harriet Devine. "Margaret Atwood: Taking the Capital W off Women." *Diverse Voices: Essays on 20th Century Women Writers in English.* Ed. Harriet Devine Jump. New York: Harvester Wheatsheaf, 1991. 98-121.

Klein, Josef, and Ulla Fix, eds. *Textbeziehungen: linguistische und literaturwissenschaftliche Beiträge zur Intertextualität.* Tübingen: Stauffenburg, 1997.

Klooß, Wolfgang. "From Colonial Madness to Postcolonial Ex-Centricity: A Story about Stories of Identity Construction in Canadian Historiographic (Meta-) Fiction." *Historiographic Metafiction in Modern American and Canadian Literature.* Eds. Bernd Engler and Kurt Müller. Paderborn: Schöningh, 1994. 53-79.

Kolodny, Anette. "Margaret Atwood and the Politics of Narrative." *Studies on Canadian Literature: Introductory and Critical Essays.* Ed. Arnold E. Davidson. New York: MLA, 1990. 90-109.

Kuester, Martin. *Framing Truths: Parodic Structures in Contemporary English-Canadian Historical Novels.* Toronto: U of Toronto P, 1992.

Leask, Nigel. "Kubla Khan and Orientalism: The Road to Xanadu Revisited". *Romanticism: The Journal of Romantic Culture and Criticism.* 1988 (4:1): 1-21.

Lecker, Robert. "Janus through the Looking Glass: Atwood's First Three Novels." Davidson & Davidson 177-203.

Ljunberg, Christina. *To Join, to Fit, and to Make: The Creative Craft of Margaret Atwood's Fiction*. Bern: Lang, 1999.

Lodge, David. *Modern Criticism and Theory: A Reader*. London: Longman, 1991.

Lomax, Marion. "Gendered Writing and the Writer's Stylistic Identity." *Essays and Studies [E&S]* 47 (1994): 1-19.

Mahoney, Elisabeth. "Writing So to Speak: The Feminist Dystopia." Sceats & Cunningham 29-40.

Mars-Jones, Adam. "Where Women Grow on Trees," *Guardian Unlimited* <http://books.guardian.co.uk/reviews/generalfiction/0,6121,369220,00.html>.

Martin, Bryan. *The Nineteenth Century (1798-1900)*. Macmillan Anthologies of English Literature, Vol. 4. London: Macmillan, 1989.

Maclean, Susan. "*Lady Oracle*: The Art of Reality and the Reality of Art." *Journal of Canadian Fiction* 28-29 (1980): 179-97.

McCombs, Judith. "Atwood's Haunted Sequences: *The Circle Game*, *Journals of Susanna Moodie*, and *Power Politics*." Davidson & Davidson 35-54.

McCracken, Scott. *Pulp: Reading Popular Fiction*. Manchester: Manchester UP, 1998.

McGlathery, James M. *Fairy Tale Romance: The Grimms, Basile, and Perrault*. Urbana: U of Illinois P, 1991.

McMillan, Ann. "The Transforming Eye: *Lady Oracle* and the Gothic Tradition." VanSpanckeren and Castro 48-64.

Miller, Nancy K. "Emphasis Added: Plots and Plausibilities in Women's Fiction." *PMLA* 96 (1981): 36-48.

Molke, Thomas. "Der Didomythos in der englischsprachigen Literatur." *Dido und Aeneas*. Ed. Gerhard Binder. Trier: WVT, 2000. 229-50.

Moss, John, ed. *Future Indicative: Literary Theory and Canadian Literature*. Ottawa: U of Ottawa P, 1987.

Müller (1997), Beate, ed. Introduction. *Parody: Dimensions and Perspectives*. Amsterdam: Rodopi. 1-10.

--- (1994). *Komische Intertextualität: Die literarische Parodie*. Trier: WVT.

Murphy, Eileen. "The Blind Assassin."
<http://www.citypaper.com/2000-11-22/imprint4.html>.

Mycak, Sonia. *In Search of the Split Subject: Psychoanalysis, Phenomenology, and the Novels of Margaret Atwood*. Toronto: ECW, 1996.

Newton, K. M. *Twentieth-Century Literary Theory: A Reader.* London: Macmillan, 1997.

Nicholson, Colin. *Margaret Atwood: Writing and Subjectivity; New Critical Essays.* Basingstoke: Macmillan, 1994.

Niederhoff, Burkhard. "How to Do Things with History: Researching Lives in Carol Shield's *Swann* and Margaret Atwood's *Alias Grace*." *JCL* 35.2 (2000): 71-85.

Nischik, Reingard M. *Mentalstilistik: Ein Beitrag zu Stiltheorie und Narrativik; dargestellt am Erzählwerk Margaret Atwoods.* Tübingen: Narr, 1991.

Parker, Emma. "You Are What You Eat: The Politics of Eating in the Novels of Margaret Atwood." *TCL* 41.3 (1995): 349-68.

Patton, Marilyn. "*Lady Oracle*: The Politics of the Body." *Ariel* 22.4 (1991): 29-48.

Perry, Kathleen Anne. *Metamorphosis and the Imagination in the Poetry of Ovid, Petrarch, and Ronsard.* New York: Lang, 1990.

Pfister (1991), Manfred. "How Postmodern Is Intertextuality?" *Intertextuality.* Ed. Heinrich F. Plett. Berlin: Walter de Gruyter, 1991. 207-24.

Pfister (1985). "Konzepte der Intertextualität." Broich and Pfister 1-30.

Postgate, J.N. *Early Mesopotamia: Society and Economy at the Dawn of History.* London: Routledge, 1992.

Quinn, Kenneth. *Virgil's Aeneid: A Critical Description.* Michigan: U of Michigan P, 1968.

Radway (1997), Janice A. *Reading the Romance: Women, Patriarchy, and Popular Literature.* Chapel Hill: U of North Carolina P.

--- (1981). "The Utopian Impulse in Popular Literature: Gothic Romances and 'Feminist' Protest." *American Quarterly* 33 (1981): 140-62.

Reinfandt, Christoph. "The Evolution of Romanticism: High Art vs. Popular Culture in Tennyson's 'The Lady of Shalott'." *Proceedings of the Conference of the German Association of University Teachers of English.* Ed. Fritz-Wilhelm Neumann and Sabine Schülting. Trier: WVT, 1999. 307-25.

Reynolds, Margaret, and Jonathan Noakes. *Margaret Atwood: The Essential Guide to Contemporary Literature.* London: Vintage, 2002.

Rogerson, Margaret. "Reading the Patchworks in *Alias Grace*." *JCL* 33.1 (1998): 5-22.

Schall, Birgitta. *Von der Melancholie zur Trauer: Postmoderne Text- und Blickökonomien bei Margaret Atwood.* Trier: WVT, 1995.

Schier, Helga. *Going Beyond: The Crisis of Identity and Identity Models in Contemporary American, English and German Fiction.* Tübingen: Niemeyer, 1993.

Sceats, Sarah, and Gail Cunningham. *Image and Power: Women in Fiction in the Twentieth Century.* London: Longman, 1996.

Selden et. al. (1997): Selden, Raman, Peter Widdowson, and Peter Brookner. *A Reader's Guide to Contemporary Literary Theory.* London: Prentice Hall, 1997.

Showalter, Elaine. "Margaret Atwood's *The Blind Assassin*." Rpt. in Reynolds & Noakes 142-3.

Solms, Wilhelm. *Die Moral von Grimms Märchen.* Darmstadt: Primus, 1999.

Staels, Hilde. *Margaret Atwood's Novels: A Study of Narrative Discourse.* Tübingen: Francke, 1995.

Stein, Karen F. "A Left-Handed Story: *The Blind Assassin*." Wilson (2003a): 135-153.

Stocker, Peter. *Theorie der intertextuellen Lektüre: Modelle und Fallstudien.* Paderborn: Schöningh, 1998.

Thomas, Clara. "*Lady Oracle*: The Narrative of a Fool-Heroine." Davidson & Davidson 159-75.

Thieme, John. "A Female Houdidni: Popular Culture in Margaret Atwood's *Lady Oracle*." *Kunapipi* 14.1 (1992): 71-80.

Underwood, Mick. "Reception Studies – Romantic Fiction." updated 21 June 3003 <http://www.cultsock.ndirect.co.uk/MUHome/cshtml/index.html>.

VanSpanckeren, Kathryn. Introduction. VanSpanckeren and Castro xix-xxvii.

VanSpanckeren, Kathryn and Jan Garden Castro, eds. *Margaret Atwood: Vision and Forms.* Carbondale: Southern Illinois UP, 1988.

Vespermann, Susanne. *Margaret Atwood: Eine Mythokritische Analyse ihrer Werke.* Augsburg: Wißner, 1995.

Viner, Katharine. "Double Bluff." *Guardian Unlimited* <http://books.guardian.co.uk/departments/generalfiction/story>.

Waugh, Patricia. *Metafiction.* London: Routledge, 1993.

Wertheimer, Jürgen. *Don Juan und Blaubart: Erotische Serientäter in der Literatur.* München: Beck, 1999.

Wilson (2003), Sharon Rose, ed. *Margaret Atwood's Textual Assassinations: Recent Poetry and Fiction*. Columbus: Ohio State UP.

--- (1996), Sharon Rose. "Atwood's Intertextual and Sexual Politics." *Approaches to Teaching Atwood's* The Handmaid's Tale *and Other Works*. Eds. Sharon R. Wilson, Thomas B. Friedman, and Shannon Hengen. New York: MLA, 1996. 55-62.

--- (1993). *Margaret Atwood's Fairy-Tale Sexual Politics*. Jackson: U of Mississippi P.

Wolf, Werner. *Ästhetische Illusion und Illusionsdurchbrechung in der Erzählkunst: Theorie und Geschichte mit Schwerpunkt auf englischem illusionsstörenden Erzählen*. Tübingen: Niemeyer, 1993.

Woodcock, George. "Bashful but Cold: Notes on Margaret Atwood as Critic." Davidson & Davidson 223-41.

Worton, Michael, and Judith Still, eds. *Intertextuality: Theories and Practices*. Manchester: Manchester UP, 1990.

Zimmermann, Jutta. *Metafiktion im Anglokanadischen Roman der Gegenwart*. Trier: WVT, 1996.

Zipes, Jack David, ed. *The Oxford Companion to Fairy Tales*. Oxford: Oxford UP, 2000.

ibidem-Verlag
Melchiorstr. 15
D-70439 Stuttgart

info@ibidem-verlag.de

www.ibidem-verlag.de
www.edition-noema.de
www.autorenbetreuung.de

www.ingramcontent.com/pod-product-compliance
Lightning Source LLC
Chambersburg PA
CBHW070737230426
43669CB00014B/2485